Taxation and Regulation of the Savings and Loan Industry

Taxation and Regulation of the Savings and Loan Industry

Kenneth R. Biederman
City Federal Savings and Loan

John A. Tuccillo
Georgetown University

Lexington Books
D. C. Heath and Company
Lexington, Massachusetts
Toronto

Material in chapters 2 and 4 of this book is drawn from K. R. Biederman and J. A. Tuccillo, *The Taxation of Financial Intermediaries: Summary Report,* © 1975, National Savings and Loan League, Washington, D.C. Reprinted with permission.

Library of Congress Cataloging in Publication Data

Biederman, Kenneth R
    Taxation and regulation of the savings and loan industry.

    Bibliography: p.
    Includes index.
    1. Building and loan associations—Taxation—United States. 2. Financial institutions—Taxation—United States. I. Tuccillo, John A., joint author. II. Title.
HG1768.U5B52   336.2′78′332320973   76-15853
ISBN 0-669-00782-x

Published simultaneously in Canada

Printed in the United States of America

International Standard Book Number: 0-669-00782-x

Library of Congress Catalog Card Number: 76-15853

To Meg and Sherry

Contents

List of Figures

List of Tables

Preface

Proponents of financial reform have repeatedly stressed that the tax aspects of such reform must, among other things, place competing financial institutions on an equal tax footing. A major aspect of the changes in the federal tax treatment of financial institutions which occurred in the Revenue Acts of 1962 and the Tax Reform Act of 1969 was that these changes were instigated essentially in the name of tax equity among commercial banks, savings and loan associations, and mutual savings banks. The notion of tax equity among competing intermediaries seems to have been the sole underlying motive behind all major tax legislation affecting these institutions over the past fifteen to twenty years, with the question of impact on housing funds flows being of secondary, and declining, importance. This book looks at the federal income taxation of these three financial intermediaries under a basic premise that questions of tax equity and fairness among financial institutions cannot be assessed without consideration of differences in regulation in what is a highly regulated industry. Our work focuses on savings and loan associations with respect to federal taxation and regulation of that industry, with an eye toward reform both within the S&L business and among closely competing intermediaries. Accordingly, our analysis is principally in relative terms. Absolute tax and regulatory burdens of savings and loan associations impart little meaning unless put on a comparable basis with other organizations.

The tax equity issue among competing intermediaries has particular significance in that the Congress is in the midst of considering major reforms in the taxation and regulation of the financial sector. The current thrust was generated by the report of the Presidential Commission on Financial Structure and Regulation in 1971 and the subsequent legislative initiatives of the Nixon and Ford administrations. The dominant idea is that all intermediaries should be treated equally with respect to both investment and liability powers, and taxation. While it is hard to quarrel with such goals, there is still a great deal of confusion as to how currently proposed legislation would move toward them.

In this book, we look at the tax reform proposals currently under congressional consideration within the equity framework.

We analyze the impact of the proposed shift in the tax structure on savings and loan associations now, and for the next four years, in an effort to provide information to the policy-making process. Our analysis is limited to the current portfolio structure of savings and loan associations, but uses individual firm data on one thousand savings and loan associations to give a firm-by-firm picture of the impact of the tax reform measures.

This book is part of a larger study commissioned by the National Savings and Loan League. That study examined in detail the manner in which savings and loan associations, commercial banks, and mutual savings banks have been and are being taxed and regulated. Our findings indicate that current attempts to restructure the tax and regulatory system to promote equity among competing financial intermediaries move in that direction, but do not go far enough to complete that particular job, at least not within the existing regulatory framework. Liberal portfolio powers allowed commercial banks relative to S&Ls have permitted banks to reduce their federal tax butdens below that of thrifts, irrespective of special industry tax privileges. Accordingly, without regulatory reforms, it is impossible for any tax reform measures to attain permanent tax equity among competing financial intermediaries.

Our thanks go to Henry Carrington and the members of the National Savings and Loan League for their support of our research and their patient ear to our findings. We are grateful to Mary Morris of the National League staff who provided liaison and administrative aid, and to Mrs. Beverly Gladd who patiently and efficiently typed our manuscripts. Research assistance was ably provided by three of our students at Georgetown—Reid Nagle, Gary Lape, and Jay Lynch. Data used in the projections of chapter 4 were provided by the Federal Home Loan Bank Board through Harris Friedman and prepared by Francis Paul. We owe a special debt of gratitude to our colleague, George Viksnins, who was a partner in the research reported in the early sections of chapter 4 and was always available for comment on the other phases of the project. In addition, we received useful comments from Edward Kane, Stanley Surrey, and Gerard Brannon. The authors wish to thank all those who helped in the preparation of this book, without implicating them in any error therein.

Taxation and Regulation of the Savings and Loan Industry

1 Introduction

The subject of federal income taxation is one that occupies a great deal of the public consciousness, especially of those charged with creating legislation. Each year the Congress turns its attention to finding ways and means of making the process of revenue generation simpler and fairer. Over the years, the annual struggle with the public purse has spawned a series of beliefs which, true or false, seem to have come down as "conventional wisdom." Such ideas as the merit of home ownership, the necessity of a strong domestic energy industry, and the role of the federal government in assisting the borrowing activities of state and local governments are reflected in the tax system as exemptions or subsidies to make these activities cost less or yield more.

Of all the industries which have been singled out in the Tax Code for particular treatment, the one that seems to reap the greatest benefits but to receive the least attention from reformers is the financial services industry. The specialized nature of thrifts as housing lenders has been consistently recognized in the tax (and regulatory) codes, with their specialized activity fostered through preferential tax treatment. Lately, increasing emphasis has been placed on the role of thrifts as intermediaries similar to commercial banks, so that equity-based changes in the tax laws have worked against thrifts in their role as housing intermediaries. However, up to now, these changes in federal taxation have not been accompanied by changes in the regulatory structure which would give thrifts the same powers as commercial banks.

Thus, there currently exists a kind of schizophrenic treatment of thrift institutions, with the tax structure moving to acknowledge the full financial intermediary status of these institutions and the regulatory system having yet to grant the powers of that status. The disintermediation of the sixties and early seventies is partially traceable to this, with the thrifts caught up in a lending long, borrowing short dilemma characteristic of periods of monetary tightness. A recognition of this situation facing thrifts was the key element in the Hunt Commission proposals of 1971, which, for the

1

most part, have been incorporated into the Financial Institutions Acts of 1973 and 1975. These proposals would tend to equalize both the powers and tax treatment of thrifts and commercial banks and establish equal treatment of what, under these provisions, would essentially be competing intermediaries.

In attempting to draw comparisons among intermediaries on equity grounds as to the impact of existing or proposed tax policy, it is essential that a basis for comparison be established which is common to all parties involved. Thus, in evaluating whether or not a given tax policy is equitable in its impact among taxpayers, a concept of equality must first be determined. Economic income is such a concept and by making comparisons among taxpayers as to effective tax rates, based upon this notion, something can be said about the nature of a tax program from an equity standpoint.

The notion of economic income has several dimensions, and it is rare that the concept is developed with respect to all of them. Economic income is usually defined as consumption plus changes in net worth from period to period, less expenses associated with generating these income flows. While it is a relatively straightforward process to apply this definition to the calculation of explicit income flows subject to current taxation, a full rendering requires going beyond traditional analyses to take into account other aspects of income flows.

The first has to do with items of tax deferral or exclusion, such as deductions for loss reserves, tax-exempt interest exclusions, investment tax credits, and so forth.

A second aspect bearing on the measurement of economic income resulting from the activities of financial intermediaries involves the relative costs and benefits of regulation. These considerations must enter into any analysis of tax equity, since, in effect, regulations represent implicit taxes or subsidies of doing business as a particular type of intermediary. Accordingly, in deriving estimations of effective tax rates for purposes of tax equity analysis, explicit compensation must be made in recognition of the regulatory process. An analysis which stresses the equity issue in the federal tax treatment of S&Ls vis-à-vis that of banks should be concerned with the effects of regulation imposed by the Federal Reserve System, the Federal Home Loan Bank System, the FDIC and FSLIC upon the economic income of the respective intermediaries, and as such, their effective tax burdens.

Regulations restrict financial intermediaries largely by defining allowable asset holdings, either by requiring holdings of a given amount of a certain asset or by prohibiting or restricting the holding of certain assets. Such restrictions impose costs on the intermediary by forcing it to hold assets which it might not otherwise hold (due to lower yields), or to forego the holding of assets it may wish to hold in its portfolio (due to higher yields). These costs can be measured by the difference in return between the actual portfolio and an "ideal" portfolio, that is, one that could prudently be held in the absence of regulation.

Costs of regulation, however, are partially offset by the benefits that accrue to a regulated intermediary. To the extent that regulation stems from membership in any of the organizations mentioned previously, the regulated intermediary also receives services as part of that membership. The benefits are generally in the form of access to borrowing facilities and funds transfer mechanisms at no cost, or at costs substantially below market prices. This price difference can be identified as a direct monetary benefit to the regulated intermediary. To be accurate, a definition of economic income must include the benefits of regulation as income and net out the costs of regulation as an extraordinary expense.

This study focuses on savings and loan associations, although questions of tax equity among competing financial intermediaries necessarily involve discussion of commercial and mutual savings banks as well. This effort attempts to place the tax and regulatory treatment of S&Ls into a single package, stressing the point that equity in taxation can be discussed only when regulatory differences have been neutralized, and vice versa.

In the following chapter, we look at the current system under which savings and loan associations are taxed at the federal level. Attention is given to issues surrounding the bad-debt deduction, which is the primary way in which S&Ls have been able to reduce their federal tax burdens since 1951, when they lost their tax-exempt status. Specifically, the analysis concentrates on the minimum portfolio percentage limitation and the 6 percent fill-up limitation under the provisions of the bad-debt deduction allowance. The implications of these restrictions on the future tax picture of S&Ls are detailed, particularly within the context of their impact on the construct of S&L portfolios. The chapter concludes with a discussion and analysis of the minimum tax, enacted as part of the Tax Reform Act of 1969, as it impacts the federal taxation of S&Ls.

The third chapter takes up the issue of the relationship between the tax and regulatory systems as they affect the tax-paying ability of S&Ls. By analyzing the effects of regulation on the income-earning potential of competing institutions in general, and S&Ls in particular, it is possible to incorporate regulatory considerations into a tax structure. We do this by redefining economic income measures to include the impact of regulation on the effective tax burdens of different intermediaries. Regulatory benefits which accrue to one intermediary relative to another are treated as income subsidies, while relative regulatory costs are treated within the context of costs of doing business. The chapter concludes with a comparison of tax burdens of thrifts and banks by the conventional means of effective rate calculation and by revised methods which account for regulatory impact.

The fourth chapter takes a rather detailed look at the matter of reform of the federal tax treatment of savings and loan associations, focusing on the notion of the mortgage tax credit as in the Financial Institutions Acts of 1973 and 1975. Using a random sample data set of S&L performance records, provided by the Federal Home Loan Bank Board, we conducted comparative analyses and projections based on a number of alternative tax scenarios which incorporate the bad-debt allowance and mortgage tax credit provisions. It is clearly demonstrated that under most economic conditions, the mortgage tax credit concept as developed within the Financial Institutions Acts would reduce S&L federal taxes compared to the existing tax structure and, accordingly, would bring the tax burden of thrifts closer to that of commercial banks. We conclude by raising the question, through some preliminary analysis and calculations, of how effective the proposed mortgage tax credit would be from the standpoint of stimulating funds flows into residential housing.

2

Issues in the Current Tax Treatment of Savings and Loan Associations

An Overview of the Federal Taxation of S&Ls

Prior to the Revenue Act of 1951, savings and loan associations, as well as mutual savings banks, were exempt from federal income taxation under the premise that since these institutions played an important role in the high national priority of financing residential construction, they should be exempt from taxation. As mutual organizations, more closely resembling nonprofit organizations than profit-oriented stock associations such as commercial banks, they seemed further to merit this preferential treatment in the eyes of the Congress. With the continuing growth of the industry and associated cries of tax equity and "fair-share" payments by the commercial banking system, Congress terminated, in the Revenue Act of 1951, the tax-exempt status of these savings institutions, thereafter recognizing their status as that of private corporate, profit-oriented organizations. But having established this distinction in the Internal Revenue Code of 1939, Congress promptly provided de facto exemption from federal income tax by permitting a most liberal allowance for bad-debt reserves. Under this proviso, savings institutions were permitted to deduct up to 100 percent of taxable income, subject to ceiling limitations on reserve accumulations, which proved to be virtually inoperative. Consequently, federal income taxes for savings institutions remained almost nonexistent until passage of the Revenue Act of 1962.

With the passage of this act, Congress legislated major changes in the tax treatment of savings and loan associations, the significance of these changes apparent from the quantum leap between 1962 and 1963 in federal income taxes paid by the industry. The Revenue Act of 1962 ended the virtual tax-exempt status of the savings and loan industry by drastically altering the definition bad-debt reserves for tax purposes. In addition, and certainly of equal importance, the 1962 act made major changes in the definitional regulations of savings and loan institutions, specifically restricting their portfolio allowances and operational activities.

5

Under the 1962 act, the 1951 statute was amended in order to provide for a bad-debt deduction allowance equal to either 60 percent of taxable income or to the amount necessary in order to increase the reserve on qualified real property to 3 percent of such loans (referred to as the "3 percent method"). Savings and loan institutions, in order to qualify for the bad-debt allowance, were required to hold at least 72 percent of their assets in qualifying nonrealty assets (cash, U.S. Government obligations, passbook loans) plus qualified realty (loans relating to residential or real church property). As an additional portfolio restriction, at least 60 percent of the assets of the S&Ls had to consist of qualifying nonrealty assets plus loans relating to residential property of one- to four-family units. Failure to meet these portfolios specifications resulted in corresponding percentage reductions in the bad-debt deduction allowance under the percentage-of-taxable-income method for determining the deduction.

The Revenue Act of 1962 primarily affected the savings and loan industry, leaving mutual savings banks virtually untouched. Most savings and loan associations were forced to use the 60-percent method of determining their bad-debt allowances, thereby paying tax upon 40 percent of taxable income. This, in turn, raised the effective tax rate from earlier levels of 1 percent to around 15 to 16 percent of economic income.[a] Mutual savings banks, on the other hand, continued to remain relatively free of federal income tax burdens, paying effective rates from 3 to 6 percent in the years after the 1962 Revenue Act and prior to enactment of the 1969 Tax Reform Act (see table 2–1). Because portfolio restrictions imposed upon savings and loan associations were not applicable to the mutual savings banks, the latter were able to take advantage of income from tax-exempt sources (such as state and local securities) and still avail themselves of a sizable bad-debt deduction through the alternative "3 percent of real property loans" method. The elimination of the 3 percent method by the 1969 Tax Reform Act, coupled with tightening of restrictions of portfolio holdings, the minimum tax, and dividend deductions allowed mutual savings banks, have raised sizably the effective rates paid by these institu-

---

[a] Economic income, as is normally defined in such rate calculations, essentially amounts to taxable income plus (1) bad-debt deductions in excess of experience; (2) tax-exempt interest; (3) net operating loss carry-overs; and (4) 85 percent of domestic dividends received. Consequently, these figures have not been adjusted in order to reflect regulatory differences.

Table 2–1

Rates of Federal Income Tax as Percentage of Economic Income, Unadjusted;[a] Mutual Savings Banks, Savings and Loan Associations, and Commercial Banks, 1955–1974

Year	(1) Commercial Banks (in percentages)	(2) S&Ls (in percentages)	(3) MSBs (in percentages)
1955	34.2%	1.6%	1.4%
1956	33.8	1.7	0.9
1957	38.3	1.5	0.6
1958	36.0	1.6	0.8
1959	34.2	1.2	0.6
1960	37.8	1.0	0.7
1961	35.6	0.8	0.6
1962	33.3	0.9	1.1
1963	30.6	16.0	2.2
1964	28.2	14.8	2.7
1965	23.3	15.2	3.4
1966	23.2	16.9	5.6
1967	22.2	13.0	4.7
1968	22.4	18.5	6.2
1969	21.3	15.5	6.4
1970	23.5	18.9	13.2
1971	20.9	21.5	15.7
1972	17.9	23.5	18.5
1973	16.1	24.7	19.3
1974	15.5	26.4	20.3

[a]Unadjusted for consideration of regulatory differences.

Sources: Internal Revenue Service, *Statistics of Income* (Source Book); Federal Home Loan Bank Board, *Combined Financial Statements*; FDIC, *Annual Reports*.

tions, although available estimates indicate they still enjoy preferential rates relative to savings and loan institutions.

The Tax Reform Act of 1969 (TRA) further decreased the bad-debt deduction provisions permitted savings and loans although the bad-debt deduction continues to be the only major tax avoidance mechanism available to them. Under current tax provisions, an association may choose to tie its bad-debt reserve additions to taxable income, experience, or percentage of eligible loans. Of the three, the percentage-of-taxable-income method is by far the most widely used.[b] The TRA reduces the 60 percent deduction permitted for the taxable income method by the Revenue Act of 1962 in scheduled steps, from 60 percent in 1969 to 40 percent in

[b] In 1973, close to 90 percent of all associations used this method for calculating additions to their loss reserves for tax purposes.

1979. To be eligible for the maximum allowance, an association must now have 82 percent or more of its portfolio in "qualifying assets,"[c] consisting of:

1. Cash;
2. U.S. government obligations;
3. Residential real property loans;
4. Loans secured by members' deposits;
5. Loans secured by church, school, health and welfare facilities, or commercial property located in an urban renewal or model cities area;
6. Student loans; or
7. Property used in the conduct of the institution's business.

For every 1 percent of an S&L portfolio in which qualified assets are below 82 percent, the bad-debt allowance is reduced by three-quarters of 1 percent. In addition to this provision, any association choosing the percentage-of-taxable-income method of calculating reserve additions may not maintain a total volume of bad-debt reserves in excess of an amount equal to 6 percent of its qualified real property loans (the 6 percent fill-up limitation). When an association reaches or exceeds this ceiling, its percentage deduction for bad-debt reserves effectively becomes zero. Both the declining percentage deduction and the 6 percent ceiling imply that under the TRA, tax rates for associations using the percentage-of-taxable-income method of calculating reserves will rise in the future. This is further intensified by the minimum tax levied on bad-debt reserves in excess of experience. Each of these provisions serves to limit the opportunity available to savings and loan associations for tax reduction and is discussed in greater detail in the following sections.

The Minimum Portfolio Percentage Limitation

The minimum portfolio percentage serves as an asset limitation which necessitates the earning of higher returns on nonqualified

---

[c] In 1974, 84.5 percent of total assets of all insured savings and loan associations were in mortgage loans and contracts, and 8.6 percent were in cash and investment securities; general reserves, surplus, and permanent stock in the aggregate stood at 6.2 percent of savings capital.

assets held by savings and loan associations than those held by commercial banks. As an example of this, consider the following:

1. Assume the applicable bad-debt deduction to be 40 percent for fully qualified savings and loan associations,[d] with a reduction of 0.75 percent for each 1 percent qualified assets fall short of 82 percent of total assets.
2. Let $\bar{X}$ represent the portfolio of a savings and loan association with a net return of X.[e] $\bar{X}$ consists of at least 82 percent qualified assets.
3. Let $\bar{Y}$ represent an alternative portfolio, available to the same savings and loan, with net return of Y. $\bar{Y}$ consists of 81 percent qualified assets.

The aftertax yield on portfolio $\bar{X}$ (which we designate as X') may be calculated as:

$$X' = X - [0.48(X - 0.4X)] \qquad (2.1)$$
$$= X - 0.228X$$
$$= 0.712X$$

We can similarly calculate the aftertax return on portfolio $\bar{Y}$. However, since $\bar{Y}$ does not contain 82 percent qualified assets, the applicable bad-debt allowance must be reduced from 40 percent to 39.25 percent (portfolio Y falls 1 percent short of the required 82 percent, so the bad-debt allowance is reduced by 0.75 percent). If we designate Y' as the aftertax return on portfolio $\bar{Y}$, then:

$$Y' = Y - [0.48(Y - 0.3925Y)] \qquad (2.2)$$
$$= Y - 0.2916Y$$
$$= 0.7084Y$$

Clearly, the aftertax return on the fully qualified portfolio is higher (given the same pretax return) than on the less than fully qualified portfolio, due to the structure of the tax law. Put another way, the savings and loan that wishes to adjust its portfolio to include more nonqualified assets will lose some tax benefits. The implication is

---

[d] The allowance specified in the TRA for 1979 scheduled full phase-in of the bad-debt provisions of TRA.

[e] Net return before tax and before the bad-debt deduction.

that it is "locked-in" to its portfolio unless it can find a nonqualified asset whose yield is higher than a qualified asset by enough to compensate for the higher taxes it will be paying.

Thus, the question is: By how much must the before-tax return on the nonqualified asset exceed the before-tax return on the qualified asset in order to fully compensate the savings and loan? This implies that X' must equal Y' or:

$$0.712X = 0.7084Y \qquad (2.3)$$

Therefore:

$$Y = (0.712/0.7084)X = 1.005082X \qquad (2.4)$$

This relationship may be further developed by a specific example. Assume that the gross yield on $\overline{X}$ (the yield before expenses are paid, which we designate as X'') is $100 and the institution must pay interest and other expenses of $80. This means that the before-tax yield on the fully qualified portfolio (X) is $20 and the yield on portfolio $\overline{Y}$ must be $20.1016 ($1.005082X$—see above) in order to provide the same aftertax yield. Accordingly, the yield on Y must equal $100.1016 in order for the aftertax returns on the two portfolios to be the same. Expressed another way, the switch of 1 percent of total assets from qualified to nonqualified assets requires that the nonqualified asset have a gross yield 10.16 percent higher than the qualified asset. Otherwise, the switch will reduce aftertax income. Thus, if qualified assets yield a gross return of 8 percent, a fully substitutable, nonqualified asset must yield 8.8128 percent.

This analysis points up an essential feature of the tax law: savings and loan associations can avail themselves of tax reduction by locking themselves into a given portfolio. If they choose to ignore the 82 percent asset requirement, they must compensate for the lost tax saving by a higher yield on the alternative asset. The implication of this is clear: if market forces determine that certain nonqualified assets are more attractive than qualified assets, the savings and loan (and mutual savings bank) can acquire these assets only at a cost which is greater than if a commercial bank were to do the same thing. Putting this another way, the yield on the nonqualified asset has to be greater for a thrift than for a commercial bank, under the conditions of this example, in order for both to do equally well in aftertax return.

The "6 Percent Fill-up"

The 6 percent fill-up clause affects the capacity of savings and loan associations to take advantage of the bad-debt deduction. If the asset growth of an association slows or disappears, it would eventually, through accretions to bad-debt reserves, lose its access to the percentage-of-taxable-income, bad-debt allowance (BDA).[f] We tested this process by conducting a series of simulations which would project tax rates for savings and loan associations over a five-year period.

The data base for our calculations is a sample of one thousand associations provided by the Federal Home Loan Bank Board. These data include detailed income, asset, liability, and tax figures based upon the actual performance of these associations in 1973. For each of the associations, we projected balance sheet performance over the remaining period of the phase-in of the TRA, 1975–79. During this period, the BDA is to be reduced from 45 percent to 40 percent of net income. To explore several alternative future environments, we have done our projections under a number of different assumptions about the growth pattern of assets and the income performance of our sample associations. With respect to asset growth, we employ the following assumptions:

1. No asset growth over the five-year period. This is chosen to reflect an extremely pessimistic scenario, but one that some associations have recently experienced.

2. Asset growth at a 5 percent annual rate over the period. This is chosen to reflect a series of "bad" (but not unreasonably bad) performance years; and,

3. Asset growth at an 11 to 12 percent annual rate over the period. This is chosen to reflect a series of reasonably "good" years. This figure also reflects asset growth in 1972–73.

Our income assumptions are also drawn from the performance of the savings and loan industry. The years 1970 and 1973 are generally considered "bad" and "good" years, respectively. During 1973, associations earned an average return of 1.1 percent on assets *net of all costs including interest*. Hence, this year is chosen as our high-income benchmark and the 1.1 percent return on assets

---

[f] Unless otherwise stated, all references hereafter to the bad-debt deduction, or allowance, are to the percentage-of-taxable-income method.

is used to generate figures for our high-income simulations. Similarly, in 1970, associations earned on the average only 0.5 percent on assets, net of all costs. Performance for this year is chosen as our low-income benchmark and the 0.5 percent figure used to generate net income for our low-income simulation.

The results of these simulations are presented in tables 2–2 to 2–4. Table 2–2 describes the current situation with respect to choice of reserve calculation method, the relationship of associations choosing the taxable income method to the 6 percent ceiling, and current tax performances. As may be noted, the overwhelming majority of associations in all size classes choose to calculate their bad-debt reserve additions by the percentage-of-taxable-income method. Hence, the declining percentage deduction under TRA and the presence of the 6 percent ceiling are relevant to the vast majority of associations. It appears, however, that the 6 percent ceiling is not a serious constraint, at least not as of 1973. No more than 5 percent of the associations in any size class were at or above the 6 percent ceiling and no more than 10 percent of any size class were above 5 percent in terms of loss reserves to qualified loans.

Table 2–2
Tax Performance of Savings and Loan Associations under Current Bad-Debt Allowance Provisions, by Asset Size of Association, 1973

Size of Assn. ($ millions)	Percentage Using Percentage of Income Reserve Calculation[a]	Percentage with Loss Reserves Over 5 Percent of Qualified Loans[b]	Percentage with Loss Reserves Over 6 Percent of Qualified Loans	Tax Rate[c]
Less than 10	82.1%	10.2%	3.0%	13.0%
10–25	87.2	10.4	0.4	18.2
25–50	88.3	6.4	NA[d]	22.5
50–100	93.0	3.8	0.75	24.7
100–250	90.7	5.7	NA	25.7
More than 250	90.0	NA	NA	26.3

[a]Percentage of associations opting for percentage-of-taxable-income method of calculating reserve additions.

[b]Percentage calculated only for associations using percentage-of-taxable-income basis of reserve calculation. Five- and 6 percent figures are ratio of total reserves against bad debt to total qualified loans at end of year.

[c]Calculated as ratio of federal taxes to net income before loss reserve deductions. No allowance made for the minimum tax or the exclusion of the first $25,000 from the 26 percent corporate surcharge.

[d]NA = less than 0.5 percent.

Source: Data from balance sheets of sample associations provided by the Federal Home Loan Bank Board.

Table 2–3
Tax Performance of Savings and Loan Associations under Bad-Debt Allowance, by Asset Size of Associations, 1975 and 1979—High Income Case

Size of Association ($ millions)	1975		1979	
	Percentage of Associations Over 6 Percent[a]	Tax Rate[b]	Percentage of Associations Over 6 Percent[a]	Tax Rate[b]
I. Zero Asset Growth[c]				
Less than 10	3.3%	26.8%	27.0%	31.9%
10–25	2.8	26.4	37.3	33.4
25–50	1.0	26.4	32.0	32.0
50–100	0.7	26.5	24.6	31.1
100–250	2.2	26.4	19.6	30.7
More than 250	0.0	26.4	30.8	32.5
II. Five Percent Asset Growth[d]				
Less than 10	3.3%	26.8%	0.7%	29.0%
10–25	0.8	26.4	0.8	29.3
25–50	NA[e]	26.4	2.5	29.0
50–100	0.7	26.5	1.4	28.8
100–250	NA	26.4	1.1	28.4
More than 250	NA	26.4	2.6	28.4
III. Twelve Percent Asset Growth[f]				
Less than 10	2.6%	26.8%	NA	28.8%
10–25	0.4	26.4	NA	28.8
25–50	NA	26.4	NA	28.8
50–100	0.7	26.5	NA	28.8
100–250	NA	26.4	NA	28.8
More than 250	NA	26.4	NA	28.8

[a]Percentage of sample associations in each size category whose reserves against bad debts exceed 6 percent of qualified assets.

[b]Calculated as ratio of tax to net income before loss reserve deductions. No allowance made for the minimum tax or the exclusion of the first $25,000 from the 26-percent corporate surcharge.

[c]Assets held constant for five years. Bad-debt allowance reduced from 45 percent to 40 percent as scheduled by Tax Reform Act of 1969.

[d]Assets grow at a 5 percent annual rate of five years. Bad-debt allowance reduced as scheduled by Tax Reform Act of 1969.

[e]NA = less than 0.5 percent.

[f]Assets grow at a 12 percent annual rate. Bad-debt allowance reduced as scheduled by Tax Reform Act of 1969.

Source: Data from balance sheets of sample associations supplied by the Federal Home Loan Bank Board. High-income case reflects industry behavior in 1973 in terms of the relation of net income to assets.

Table 2–4
Tax Performance of Savings and Loan Associations under Bad-Debt Allowance, by Asset Size of Association, 1975 and 1979—Low Income Assumption

Size of Association ($ millions)	1975		1979	
	Percentage of Associations Over 6 Percent[a]	Tax Rate[b]	Percentage of Associations Over 6 Percent[a]	Tax Rate[b]
I. Zero Asset Growth[c]				
Less than 10	3.3%	26.8%	9.2%	30.5%
10–25	0.8	26.4	10.2	30.0
25–50	NA[d]	26.4	7.0	30.0
50–100	0.7	26.5	4.4	29.5
100–250	NA	26.4	5.4	29.5
More than 250	NA	26.4	NA	28.8
II. Five Percent Asset Growth[e]				
Less than 10	2.6%	26.8%	0.7%	29.0%
10–25	0.4	26.4	NA	28.8
25–50	NA	26.4	NA	28.8
50–100	0.7	26.5	NA	28.8
100–250	NA	26.4	NA	28.8
More than 250	NA	26.4	NA	28.8
III. Twelve Percent Asset Growth[f]				
Less than 10	2.6%	26.8%	NA	28.8%
10–25	0.4	26.4	NA	28.8
25–50	NA	26.4	NA	28.8
50–100	0.7	26.5	NA	28.8
100–250	NA	26.4	NA	28.8
More than 250	NA	26.4	NA	28.8

[a]Percentage of sample associations in each size category whose reserves against bad debts exceed 6 percent of qualified assets.

[b]Calculated as ratio of tax to net income before loss reserve deductions. No allowance made for the minimum tax or the exclusion of the first $25,000 from the 26-percent corporate surcharge.

[c]Assets held constant for five years. Bad-debt allowance reduced from 45 percent to 40 percent as scheduled by Tax Reform Act of 1969.

[d]NA = less than 0.5 percent.

[e]Assets grow at a 5 percent annual rate of five years. Bad-debt allowance reduced as scheduled by Tax Reform Act of 1969.

[f]Assets grow at a 12 percent annual rate. Bad-debt allowance reduced as scheduled by Tax Reform Act of 1969.

Source: Data from balance sheets of sample associations supplied by Federal Home Loan Bank Board. Low-income case reflects industry behavior in 1970 in terms of the relation of net income to assets.

There were far more associations in the smaller asset size classes which bumped against the ceiling than in the larger classes, reflecting the more rapid growth patterns of qualified assets among larger associations than among smaller ones. To cite an example, in 1973, mortgage loans for the largest class of associations (over $250 million in assets) grew at a 13 percent rate, while those of the smallest associations (under $10 million) grew at only 7 percent. This means that the total allowable volume of bad-debt reserves under TRA grew faster for large associations than for small. In effect, the ceiling receded faster for large associations. Hence, one might expect them to be less troubled by the 6 percent limitation.

Tables 2–3 and 2–4 present our projections for 1975 and 1979 with respect to the tax performance of associations. Table 2–3 presents the results of our high-income case for all three asset assumptions, while table 2–4 describes the low-income case. In addition, we note the percentage of associations bumping or exceeding the 6 percent ceiling. Several points need to be made with respect to these results:

1. Tax rates, as might be expected, are inversely related to asset growth, regardless of income assumption. The reason for this is that with low rates of asset growth, the 6 percent ceiling comes into effect for more associations more quickly, reducing their tax deduction and increasing their tax rates. With a no-growth assumption, tax rates rise by 2.5 to 7.0 percentage points over this period, while in the 12 percent growth case, the increase is only 2 to 2.5 percentage points.

2. Generally, the tax rates are higher under the high-income assumption than under the low-income assumption, regardless of the asset growth rate assumption. This result appears to be due to the faster buildup of bad-debt reserves under the high-income assumption. Thus, the 6 percent ceiling comes into effect faster, the higher the income of an association. The differences in tax rates, however, do not appear to be significant.

3. Both of the previous contentions appear to be verified by the distribution of associations by the ratio of bad-debt reserves to qualifying assets. Under the zero-asset-growth assumption, the number of associations at the ceiling increases rather sharply between 1975 and 1979. In fact, under this most pessimistic scenario, some one-quarter to one-third of associations breach the ceiling by 1979. For our other asset assumptions, however, this is not the

case. What this means is that several successive years of low- or no-asset growth (1974?) would have severe tax consequences for S&Ls. It is interesting to note that under the high-income assumption, more associations fall at or near the ceiling than under the low-income assumption.

The tables presented here show that under the existing law with respect to the bad-debt allowance, the federal tax rates paid by associations will rise over the next five years by anywhere from 2 to 7 percentage points. Based on 1973 figures, this represents anywhere from an 8 to 50 percent increase in relative tax burdens. This becomes even more striking due to the tendency for low-income and slow-asset-growth years to coincide, as they did in 1970 and 1974. The reason for this is that the escalation of interest rates reduces asset return margins by increasing costs, particularly interest costs. In addition, high interest rates are generally associated with disintermediation and thus slow asset growth.

All of this suggests that a better alternative to the BDA might be found in the way of a home mortgage subsidy. That which has been most frequently discussed among proponents of financial institution restructuring is the mortgage tax credit. A comparative analysis of this tax provision with the existing bad-debt allowance is reserved until the fourth chapter.

The Minimum Tax

The concept of the minimum income tax is to tax those taxpayers who, due to the use of significant amounts of tax preferences, are able to lower their effective tax rates far below that which would be expected given their level of economic income. Initially proposed to Congress as a tax to be levied upon individuals, the Conference Committee Bill, which was signed into law in December 1969, contained a minimum tax provision applicable for both individuals and corporations. Basically, the tax is a flat 10 percent rate applied to the sum of certain preference items excluded from the regular income tax, less both a $30,000 exemption per taxpayer and regular income taxes net of all credits. Among those preference items included in the minimum tax which particularly affect financial institutions are three-eighths of net long-term capital gains and additions to reserves for losses on bad debts in excess of experience.

Table 2–5
Ratio of Minimum Tax to Total Federal Income Taxes and
Distribution of Regular[a] and Minimum Tax, Savings and Loan
Associations, by Asset Size

Asset Size ($1,000,000)	Ratio of Minimum Tax to Total Federal Income Taxes (%)	Ratio of Minimum Tax to Minimum Tax Paid by All S&Ls (%)	Ratio of Regular[a] Income Tax to Regular Taxes Paid by All S&Ls (%)
Under $10	1.3	0.7	5.0
$10–$25	7.2	8.4	14.2
$25–$50	10.6	15.3	17.0
$50–$100	11.8	19.4	19.2
Over $100	14.2	56.2	44.6
All associations	11.6%	100.0%	100.0%

[a]Income taxes net of the minimum tax.
Source: *Corporation Source Book of Statistics of Income*, U.S. Department of the Treasury, Internal Revenue Service.

Table 2–5 distributes the existing minimum and regular income taxes paid by savings and loan associations[g] by association size and shows the impact of the minimum tax relative to total federal income taxes paid, again by association size. It can be seen that the burden of the minimum tax, as measured by the ratio of minimum tax payments to total taxes, increases with the asset size of the association. For the industry as a whole, the minimum tax averages 11.6 percent of total taxes paid, ranging from 1.3 percent for associations with assets less than $10 million to 14.2 percent for the average association with assets in excess of $100 million. Accordingly, the minimum tax is seen to be progressive relative to the regular tax in terms of size of institution. For the larger associations ($100 million of assets and above), the minimum tax has the effect of increasing their federal tax burden relative to that of the smaller associations (assets less than $50 million). Whereas the larger associations pay 44 to 45 percent of the regular federal income tax, they pay slightly over 56 percent of the minimum tax. Consequently, the minimum tax would increase the total industry share of federal taxes borne by these associations. In striking contrast, associations with assets below $10 million pay minimum taxes at 14 percent of the rate of regular taxes.

Table 2–6 draws a comparison of selected minimum-tax items for commercial banks, savings and loan associations, and mutual

[g] 1970–71 ratios.

Table 2–6

A Comparison of Selected Minimum Tax Items: Commercial Banks, Savings and Loan Associations, and Mutual Savings Banks

Item	Commercial Banks	Savings & Loan Associations	Mutual Savings Banks
Gross Preference Income[a]	$228.3	$438.3	$70.2
Gross Preference Income as Percent of Net Income[b]	3.9%	118.0%	41.9%
Net Preference Income[c]	$ 20.1	$216.7	$36.2
Net Preference Income as Percentage of Gross Preference Income	8.8%	49.4%	51.6%
Minimum Tax[d]	$ 1.7	$ 21.4	$ 3.5
Minimum Tax as Percentage of Gross Preference Income	0.74%	4.88%	4.98%
Minimum Tax as Percentage of Total Taxes Paid	0.12%	11.60%	9.95%

[a]In millions of dollars; preference income as defined in section 57 of the Internal Revenue Code regarding the minimum tax.

[b]Receipts less deductions.

[c]In millions of dollars; gross preference income less exclusion allowance and deductions for regular taxes paid.

[d]In millions of dollars; differences in these figures and 10 percent of the corresponding entry in line 2 are due to deferred taxes resulting from carry-over provisions.

Source: Treasury Department, Internal Revenue Service, *Statistics of Income—Corporation Source Book,* Washington, D.C., 1970–72.

savings banks. Based upon the current definition of preference items for purpose of the minimum tax, commercial banks had (in 1970–71) $228 million in preference income, slightly less than 4 percent of their net income. Savings and loan associations had $438 million in preference income from excess bad-debt deductions, amounting to 118 percent of net income.[h] Like S&Ls, mutual savings banks had a sizable portion of net income classified as preference income under the provisions of the minimum tax, nearly 10 times that of commercial banks.

The 10 percent minimum tax is levied on net preference income, the difference between it and gross preference income being the exclusion allowance and the deduction for regular taxes. It can be seen from table 2–6 that banks are far more successful than either S&Ls or mutual savings banks in reducing their gross pref-

[h] Net income here consists of gross receipts less deductions, exclusive of bad-debt deductions.

erence income to a net preference income which is subject to tax. Thus, only 8.8 percent of commercial bank income which is considered preference income under Sec. 57 of the Tax Code is subject to the minimum tax. Savings and loan associations and mutual savings banks on the other hand have nearly 50 percent of their income classed as "preference income" under this provision subject to the 10 percent minimum tax.

The impact of all this on the federal taxation of the three intermediaries can be determined from the last two rows of table 2–6. The effective rate of (minimum) tax on commercial banks is less than 1 percent (0.74%), even though the statutory rate is 10 percent. As expected from our previous observations, the effective rates for both S&Ls and mutual banks is several times higher, nearly 5 percent in both cases.

The relative increase in tax burdens as a consequence of the minimum tax again has been fairly significant for S&Ls and mutual banks, increasing S&L taxes by nearly 12 percent and mutual bank taxes by 10 percent. The impact of the minimum tax on commercial bank taxes, on the other hand, has been virtually nonexistent, resulting in slightly over a one-tenth of 1 percent increase in total taxes paid.

The disproportionate impact of the minimum tax on savings and loans and mutual banks is not due to S&Ls and mutual banks having considerably more tax preferred income than commercial banks. The primary difference is due to the fact that the current minimum tax includes additions to reserves for bad debts, the primary tax preference items for S&Ls and mutual banks, but excludes the interest from state and local securities, an important tax preference income item for commercial banks (and a growing item for mutual banks as well).

In the initial version of the minimum tax, as well as the version that passed the House, interest on state and local securities was included as a preference item in the minimum-tax base, although at no time was it in the minimum tax for corporations.[i] Apart from considerations as to the impact on costs of borrowing for state and local governments,[j] there is little to support the proposition that

[i] After the House version of the minimum tax, interest on state and local securities was dropped. The notion of a minimum tax on corporations was not introduced until the Senate Finance Committee.

[j] Which in and of itself has little to do with whether or not tax-exempt interest is in fact tax-preferred income to banks, or to anyone else.

interest from these securities is not preference income and accordingly should not be subject to the minimum tax. Table 2–7 compares the present impact of the minimum tax on commercial banks with the impact of an identically structured tax which includes tax-exempt interest in the preference tax base.

Such an adjustment in the minimum tax would bring commercial banks into line with savings and loan associations, at least as concerns the tax on preference income. By including interest on tax-exempts in the gross preference base and allowing for the full deduction of regular taxes less credits, net preference income of commercial banks would equal 51.6 percent of gross preference income, exactly the same as is currently the case for mutual banks and only slightly higher than for S&Ls. The minimum tax on commercial banks would increase from $20 million to nearly $150 million, bringing the effective minimum tax rate up from 0.74 percent, to 5.16 percent, again about the same as that presently borne by S&Ls and mutual savings banks.[k] Finally, the impact of this revised minimum tax would be to increase total federal taxes of commercial banks by 10.7 percent, still marginally less than the impact of the existing minimum tax on the federal taxes of S&Ls and mutual savings banks.[1]

As has been brought out in these tables, a major impact of the minimum tax has been to aid in changing the pattern of effective tax rates which existed in 1969 between S&Ls and commercial banks. At that time commercial banks were paying federal taxes at higher effective rates; the minimum tax helped to eliminate this differential. However, since effective rates between S&Ls and commercial banks appear to have equalized in the 1970–71 period, with S&Ls currently paying at higher rates, the impact of the minimum tax is exacerbating the existing rate differential, since the gap between savings and loans and banks is widening.

An additional consideration is that both the introduction of the minimum tax and reductions in allowances for additions to reserves for bad debts in the TRA have decreased the relative attractiveness to S&Ls of holding qualified assets. In order to obtain some feel for the impact which the declining bad-debt allowance

---

[k] This 5.16 percent rate is likely to be high since no allowances were made here for the carry-over loss and carry-over tax provisions. Inclusion of tax-exempt interest in the minimum tax base of mutual banks would increase their minimum tax by $1 million, resulting in an effective minimum tax rate of 5.5 percent.

[1] Cf. Table 2–6.

Table 2–7
A Comparison of Selected Minimum Tax Items for Commercial Banks, with and without Tax-Exempt Interest Included in the Minimum Tax Base

Item	Commercial Banks	
	Without Tax-Exempt Interest in Minimum Tax Base	With Tax-Exempt Interest in Minimum Tax Base
Gross Preference Income[a]	$228.3	$2846.5
Net Preference Income[b]	$ 20.1	$1472.5
Net Preference Income as Percentage of Gross Preference Income	8.8%	51.6%
Minimum Tax[c]	$ 1.7	$ 147.2
Minimum Tax as Percentage of Gross Preference Income	0.74%	5.16%
Minimum Tax as Percentage of Total Taxes Paid	0.12%	10.7%

[a]In millions of dollars; preference income as defined in section 57 of the Internal Revenue Code regarding the minimum tax, plus tax-exempt interest in column 2.
[b]In millions of dollars; gross preference income less exclusion allowance and deductions for regular taxes paid.
[c]In millions of dollars.
Source: Treasury Department, Internal Revenue Service, *Statistics of Income— Corporation Source Book,* Washington, D.C., 1970–72.

and alternative minimum tax structures would have upon the attractiveness to savings and loan associations of qualified assets relative to nonqualified assets, we can compare the before-tax return of assets within a portfolio that qualifies for the full percentage-of-taxable-income allowance with that of assets in a nonqualified portfolio. As a benchmark, we assume that the after-tax yields of the two assets are equal.

For exemplary purposes, consider the situation of an asset that qualifies for purposes of the bad-debt reserve allowance with a before-tax, net yield of X. Let Y designate the before-tax yield on an asset held under conditions that would not qualify for purposes of the bad-debt deduction. If we assume a bad-debt allowance of 0.40 of taxable income, then the aftertax yield (X') on the holder of the qualifying asset would be $0.712X$.[m]

---

[m] $X' \times X - (X - 0.4X)(0.48)$

$X = X - 0.288X = 0.712X$;

48 percent marginal tax rate assumed.

By comparison, an asset that did not qualify for the bad-debt deduction would have an aftertax yield $Y' = 0.52Y$. Thus, if the aftertax yields are to be the same under conditions of qualification as under nonqualification, then $X = 0.73Y$;[n] that is, under the assumption of a bad-debt allowance of 40 percent of net income, then an asset that qualifies for this provision need only have a before-tax yield equal to 73 percent of that of an asset that does not qualify for this tax provision in order for their aftertax returns to be equal.

Clearly, a change in the bad-debt allowance and/or a change in the tax structure would alter this sort of relation between these assets. In order to test the sensitivity (and presumably the relative benefits) of qualification to these notions, five different levels of the bad-debt allowance are assumed for each of four different tax structures. The bad-debt allowance rates assumed under the taxable-income method of calculating reserve allowances are: 0.60, 0.51, 0.47, 0.43, and 0.40, corresponding to allowances under section 593 for 1969, 1972, 1974, 1976, and 1979 (and thereafter), respectively. The tax structures assumed are the present structure[o] with: (1) no minimum tax; (2) the present minimum tax; (3) the present minimum tax with no deduction for taxes;[p] and (4) a minimum tax with no deduction for taxes plus a 24 percent flat rate (compared to the present 10 percent rate). The results of these calculations are shown in table 2–8. Although the figures are shown in terms of ratios, they can be interpreted in terms of percents.[q] As an example, an institution that qualifies under section 593 of the IRS Code (such as an S&L) would have had to have a pretax return on its qualifying assets of only 64 percent of the pretax return on the taxable assets of a nonqualifying institution (such as a commercial bank) in order to obtain the same aftertax return on these assets, assuming 1969 levels of the bad-debt allow-

---

[n]
$$X' = Y'$$
$$0.712X = 0.52Y$$

$$\therefore X = \frac{0.52}{0.712}\, Y = 0.73Y$$

[o] 48 percent tax rate assumed with present provisions for the bad-debt allowance.

[p] The $30,000 exemption is ignored.

[q] The reader should bear in mind that comparisons of relative differences in figures are the important concept here, not necessarily the absolute values.

Table 2–8

Comparison of Before-Tax Returns on Qualifying[a] Assets to Before-Tax Returns on Nonqualifying Taxable Assets such that Aftertax Returns are Equal; for Different Levels of Bad-Debt Allowance and for Alternate Tax Structures[b]

Bad-Debt Allowance[c] (In percentage)	*Ratio of Before-Tax Yields[d]*			
	No Minimum Tax[e]	*Present Minimum Tax*	*Minimum Tax— Alternative I[f]*	*Minimum Tax— Alternative II[g]*
60%	0.643	0.678	0.695	0.783
51	0.680	0.705	0.728	0.809
47	0.697	0.720	0.744	0.822
43	0.716	0.731	0.761	0.834
40	0.730	0.742	0.774	0.844

[a]Qualification under provisions for the percentage-of-taxable-income method for determining the bad-debt deduction.

[b]48-percent tax rate assumed; for all calculations it is assumed that holders of qualifying assets qualify for the full bad-debt allowance.

[c]Deduction permitted under section 593 of IRS Code as a percentage of taxable income.

[d]Ratio of before-tax yield on qualifying assets to that on nonqualifying assets such that aftertax yields are equal.

[e]Present tax structure, no minimum tax assumed.

[f]Present minimum tax with no allowance for deduction of regular taxes paid.

[g]Present minimum tax with no allowance for deduction of taxes, plus a 24 percent flat-rate tax.

ance and no minimum tax. Consideration of the minimum tax reduces the comparative advantage such that even under continued levels of the bad-debt allowance as existed in 1969, pretax return on the qualified portfolio would only have to be 67.8 percent of the pretax return on the nonqualified portfolio in order to realize equal aftertax returns. Under full phase-in of the provisions of section 593, the pretax return on the assets of the qualifying institution would have to equal 74 percent of taxable assets held by the nonqualifying investor.

The competitive advantage of qualifying for the bad-debt allowance would continue to erode if changes in the minimum tax were enacted. For example, if the rate were increased to 24 percent and the deduction of regular taxes eliminated, the pretax return on the qualified portfolio would have to increase to nearly 85 percent of the pretax return of the nonqualifying assets in order to maintain the same aftertax return.

Table 2–9 shows the results of a similar analysis with the before-tax returns of assets of a qualified portfolio compared to returns on tax-exempt assets in a portfolio not qualifying under section 593 provisions. As evidenced therein, under the present tax structure with a current bad-debt allowance of 47 percent, the before-tax return on the qualified assets would need to be 138 percent of the before-tax return on a tax-exempt portfolio in order to yield equal returns after tax. Complete phase-in of relevant provisions of the Tax Reform Act will increase this to 143 percent. By comparison, a major change in the minimum tax similar to Alternative II would require that the before-tax return on qualified assets exceed that of tax-exempts by some 62 percent. Similar analyses and comparisons can be drawn from the table.

An alternate way of analyzing the differential impact of tax changes upon assets in qualifying vs. nonqualifying portfolios is by

Table 2–9
Comparison of Before-Tax Returns on Qualifying[a] Assets to Before-Tax Returns on Nonqualifying Tax-Exempt Assets such that Aftertax Returns are Equal; for Different Levels of the Bad-Debt Allowance and for Alternate Tax Structures[b]

	Ratio of Before Tax Yields [d]			
Bad-Debt Allowance [c] *(In percentage)*	*No Minimum Tax* [e]	*Present Minimum Tax*	*Minimum Tax— Alternative I* [f]	*Minimum Tax— Alternative II* [g]
60%	1.24	1.30	1.34	1.51
51	1.31	1.36	1.40	1.56
47	1.34	1.38	1.43	1.58
43	1.38	1.41	1.46	1.60
40	1.40	1.43	1.49	1.62

[a]Qualification under provisions for the percentage-of-taxable-income method for determining the bad-debt deduction.

[b]48-percent tax rate assumed; for all calculations it is assumed that holders of qualifying assets qualify for the full bad-debt allowance.

[c]Deduction permitted under section 593 of IRS Code as a percentage of taxable income.

[d]Ratio of before-tax yield on qualifying assets to that on nonqualifying assets such that aftertax yields are equal.

[e]Present tax structure, no minimum tax assumed.

[f]Present minimum tax with no allowance for deduction of regular taxes paid.

[g]Present minimum tax with no allowance for deduction of taxes, plus a 24 percent flat-rate tax.

measuring the extent of the tax subsidy in terms of net investment yields. As an example of this approach, consider a yield on an asset in a qualified portfolio equal to $100, with an $80 payout to depositors as a cost of investment funds[r] with a bad-debt allowance of 0.4 of taxable income. Thus, taxable income on the qualified asset would be $20. By previous analysis, before-tax income on a nonqualifying taxable asset would have to be $27.40 under these assumptions[s] in order for both assets to yield equal aftertax returns. Accordingly, the net yield from the nonqualified portfolio would have to be $107.40, compared to $100 net return on the qualified assets in order for aftertax return to be equal.[t]

Employing this approach, table 2–10 shows the net investment income of nonqualifying taxable assets in order to yield the same aftertax return as qualifying assets yielding a net return of $100. Putting some of these figures into words, a taxable asset from a nonqualified portfolio (such as that of a commercial bank) would need to have, under present tax law,[u] net earnings of $107.34 in order to have the same aftertax return as assets in a qualified portfolio (such as that of a savings and loan association) which return net earnings of $100. This compares to $111.08, which was the net return necessary in 1969, with a bad-debt allowance of 60 percent of net income and prior to the minimum tax, to bring about aftertax equity. Thus, whereas in 1969 the bad-debt provisions provided a tax subsidy to assets in qualified portfolios equivalent to an 11.08 percent increase in investment yield over nonqualifying taxable assets,[v] this subsidy has decreased to a 7.34 percent differential in investment yield. As is seen in table 2–10, the value of this subsidy to qualified portfolios would decrease substantially under Alternative II of the minimum tax to an equivalent increase in yield of only 3.7 percent in 1979.

---

[r] The actual ratio of cost of funds to net income (before deduction of cost of funds) was $79 per $100 of net income for savings and loan associations in 1974.

[s] Bad-debt allowance = 40 percent of taxable income; no minimum tax; tax rate = 48 percent.

[t] The $80 cost of funds is assumed throughout for both qualified and nonqualified portfolios.

[u] Given the previous assumptions. Present tax law here refers to a 43 percent bad-debt allowance and the existing minimum tax.

[v] Thus, an asset with an 8 percent net yield which was in a qualified portfolio would equal an asset with an 8.8864 percent $[0.08 + (0.1108)(0.08) = 0.88864 = 8.8864\%]$ net yield in a nonqualified portfolio, in terms of equal, aftertax returns.

Table 2–10

Net Investment Income Required on a Nonqualifying Taxable Asset such that the Aftertax Return is Equivalent to that of a Qualifying[a] Asset Yielding a Net Income of \$100; for Different Levels of the Bad-Debt Allowance and for Alternate Tax Structures[b]

	Net Income on Nonqualifying Asset[d]			
Bad-Debt Allowance[c] (In percentage)	No Minimum Tax[e]	Present Minimum Tax	Minimum Tax— Alternative I[f]	Minimum Tax— Alternative II[g]
60%	\$111.08	\$109.51	\$108.77	\$105.54
51	109.41	108.36	107.46	104.71
47	108.67	107.77	106.87	104.34
43	107.94	107.34	106.28	103.97
40	107.40	106.95	105.85	103.69

[a]Qualification under provisions for the percentage-of-taxable-income method for determining the bad-debt deduction.

[b]48-percent tax rate assumed; for all calculations it is assumed that holders of qualifying assets qualify for the full bad-debt allowance.

[c]Deduction permitted under section 593 of IRS Code as a percentage of taxable income.

[d]Net income required for aftertax return equal to that of a qualifying asset yielding a net income of \$100.

[e]Present tax structure, no minimum tax assumed.

[f]Present minimum tax with no allowance for deduction of regular taxes paid.

[g]Present minimum tax with no allowance for deduction of taxes, plus a 24 percent flat-rate tax.

In order to complete the comparative analysis presented in tables 2–8 and 2–9, table 2–11 presents results in a similar vein to those shown in table 2–10, with the exception that the comparisons are drawn between taxable, qualifying assets and tax-exempt, non-qualifying assets. As can be seen from this table, the relative attractiveness of tax-exempt securities to qualifying securities will, by 1979, be nearly twice that as at the time of the Tax Reform Act. Proposed changes in the minimum tax would further increase the relative attractiveness of nonqualifying tax-exempts in a manner and by relative degrees as indicated in the table.

What these tables show is that, since 1969, the competitive advantage granted qualified portfolios over nonqualified ones under the provisions of the bad-debt allowance has been steadily declining, in the nature of and by degrees as indicated in the previous calculations. Changes in the minimum tax along the lines

Table 2–11

Net Investment Income Required on a Qualifying[a] Asset such that the Aftertax Return is Equivalent to that of a Nonqualifying Tax-Exempt Asset Yielding a Net Income of $100; for Different Levels of the Bad-Debt Allowance and for Alternate Tax Structures[b]

Bad-Debt Allowance[c] (In percentage)	*Net Income Qualifying Asset[d]*			
	No Minimum Tax[e]	*Present Minimum Tax*	*Minimum Tax— Alternative I[f]*	*Minimum Tax— Alternative II[g]*
60%	$104.75	$106.06	$106.74	$110.12
51	106.15	107.13	108.02	111.13
47	106.83	107.70	108.63	111.60
43	107.53	108.14	109.27	112.09
40	108.08	108.54	109.76	112.47

[a]Qualification under provisions for the percentage-of-taxable-income method for determining the bad-debt deduction.

[b]48-percent tax rate assumed; for all calculations it is assumed that holders of qualifying assets qualify for the full bad-debt allowance.

[c]Deduction permitted under section 593 of IRS Code as a percentage of taxable income.

[d]Net income required for aftertax yield equal to that of a nonqualifying asset yielding a net income of $100.

[e]Present tax structure, no minimum tax assumed.

[f]Present minimum tax with no allowance for deduction of regular taxes paid.

[g]Present minimum tax with no allowance for deduction of taxes, plus a 24 percent flat-rate tax.

discussed herein would exacerbate this erosion process to the point that under certain circumstances the advantage of the subsidy would be negligible.

When one speaks of qualified assets within the context of qualified portfolios, one is concerned primarily with residential mortgages. To the extent that S&Ls enjoyed a competitive advantage in the holding of certain assets, such as residential mortgages, to the holding of other assets, this advantage has been reduced by the 1969 tax act. Consequently, alternative investments become increasingly attractive to such qualifying institutions.[w]

[w] In a survey of savings and loan associations, Edward Kane and John Valentini found that the effect predicted earlier was occurring during the period 1969–71. In 1969, they found that only 13.0 percent of savings and loan associations using the taxable income method for calculating additions to bad-debt reserves had qualifying assets less than the 82 percent level. By 1970 this had increased to 20.8 percent, and by 1971, to 29.4 percent. Although not

In summing up this analysis of the minimum tax as it impacts S&Ls, we reach the following conclusions:

1. In regard to the question of tax equity, the minimum tax as enacted in the Tax Reform Act of 1969 has succeeded in increasing the effective tax rates of savings and loan associations by 2 to 3 percentage points. Between competing intermediaries, the effect has been to increase the gap that currently exists between commercial banks and savings and loan associations. Increases in the minimum tax would only widen this divergence in favor of commercial banks inasmuch as they are, to a great extent, excluded from the impact of the minimum tax because a major tax preference item, income on tax-exempt securities, is not included as a preference item in the minimum-tax base. On the other hand, the primary tax preference of savings and loan associations is included in this base; namely, additions to bad-debt reserves in excess of experience. Since initially all recommended changes in the existing minimum tax involve either alterations in the rates or variations in existing exemptions or deductions, and not changes in what constitutes preference income for purposes of the tax, our analysis indicates that any pretense of either establishing or even maintaining tax equity between commercial banks and savings and loan associations by these changes is false and would in fact have just the opposite effect.

2. Neutrality considerations are more complex inasmuch as the current system is nonneutral in so many ways that it is practically impossible to conclude that any change in the tax structure is more or less neutral by comparison. However, the one overriding consequence of changes in the federal income tax structure, which has resulted from both the minimum tax and section 593, is that incentives for intermediaries to hold qualified assets, such as residential mortgages, have been reduced. Empirical evidence indicates that in fact these changes have brought about a decrease in qualified assets held by savings and loan associations, although the degree of these portfolio changes and recent experience cannot be readily assessed at this time, due to the lag in data reporting.

reporting the nature of the distribution over time of the ratio of qualified to total assets of associations below that 82 percent level, Kane and Valentini concluded that ". . . this trend has serious consequences for the mortgage market, and perhaps also for the relative after-tax profitability of federally chartered SLA's and state chartered associations. . . ."

Edward J. Kane and John Valentini, "Tax Avoidance by Savings and Loan Associations Before and After the Tax Reform Act of 1969," *Journal of Monetary Economics*, *1*, No. 1 (January 1975), pp. 41–64.

3. Finally, one must regard the minimum tax with a certain amount of skepticism. Under the guise of tax equity, the minimum tax was intended to subject to tax that income which escaped regular taxation; and in fact, as originally proposed, it would have been fairly successful in accomplishing this among individual taxpayers. However, the revision of the minimum tax which was legislated fails on the equity count in various ways. First, many preference income items which should be included in the tax base have been excluded. Second, many income items were included that are tax deferrals, not tax exemptions, with no recapture provisions. Third, the minimum tax discriminates against thrifts vis-à-vis commercial banks, an inequity that does not seem to be justifiable on the basis of the impact of the regular income tax. Fourth, the impact of the minimum tax on the mortgage market appears to conflict directly with overall congressional policy on housing. Minimum-tax legislation, which would raise the rates and reduce or eliminate existing deductions without changing preference items included in the base, would increase the incentive for thrifts to reduce residential mortgages in their portfolios without providing compensating incentive for other intermediaries to increase their holdings of such assets.

The Concept of Tax Equity

Before we turn to issues concerning the interplay of taxation and regulation of S&Ls, the tax equity concept within the context of competing financial institutions needs further clarification and detail. In tax legislative matters affecting commercial banks and thrift institutions, the practice in the past has been to compare effective tax rates of the industries in question. Essentially these calculations have involved taking the ratio of taxes paid to an adjusted net income figure called "economic income." In the case of commercial banks, MSBs, and S&Ls, this measure of economic income has been defined as taxable income, plus bad-debt deductions in excess of actual losses, tax-exempt interest, loss carry-overs, and a certain percentage of intercorporate dividends received. This measure is useful over time for reflecting relative changes in tax incidence, even though suspect as to accurately reflecting the comparative incidence of tax at any point in time. Figure 2–1 shows a time series of these effective rates for commercial banks, S&Ls,

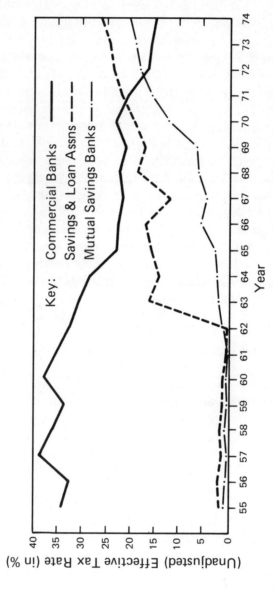

Figure 2–1. Rates of Federal Income Tax as Percentage of Economic Income, Unadjusted; Mutual Savings Banks, Savings and Loan Associations, and Commercial Banks, 1955–1974

and MSBs from 1955 through 1974. The impacts of the Revenue Act of 1962 and the Tax Reform Act of 1969 upon thrifts are clearly brought out in this figure.

Under these conventional measures, the tax burdens of commercial banks have been declining steadily since 1960, not so much as a consequence of any changes in the tax code, which favors commercial banks,[x] but rather as a result of the investment activities of banks which have resulted in steadily falling tax burdens.[1]

As to projecting figure 2–1 into the future, it appears that, due to the nature of the existing tax law, the rates for S&Ls will climb to between 28 and 30 percent by 1980.[y] As to the future of commercial bank taxation, it is almost impossible to predict how long or how far the rate decline reflected in figure 2–1 will continue. Because of the tax awareness of commercial banks and their extensive portfolio flexibility, large commercial banks have the ability to virtually eliminate any federal income tax burdens entirely; indeed, several major banks have already accomplished that feat.[2] However, we would have to agree with the observation of Edward Kane in making any prognosis of the future of the rates shown for commercial banks: continued reduction of rates such as is reflected in figure 2–1 may prove to be (politically) dangerous, involving some stringent or primitive tax action on the part of the Congress as a consequence.[3] Accordingly, we would not expect the federal tax incidence on commercial banks to continue to decline as it has been doing; rather, the rates should level off and perhaps even show slight increases.

The future impact of the current federal tax structure on mutual savings banks is somewhat uncertain because of the fact that they enjoy wider investment powers than S&Ls. Because the changes in the TRA concerning the bad-debt allowance apply to MSBs as well as to S&Ls, the similar rise in the effective tax rates of those two

---

[x] In fact, several changes in the 1969 Tax Act were specifically directed toward reducing tax avoidance opportunities available to banks.

[y] The basic assumption here is that the tax treatment of S&Ls does not change nor are there any major shifts in the makeup of their portfolios. There are, however, two important considerations in this regard. The first concerns possible increases in the minimum tax. Changes in the minimum tax which have been receiving the greatest attention by the Congress would mean a further increase in the above rates by some 2 to 3 percentage points. See Kenneth R. Biederman and John A. Tuccillo, *Equity Issues as They Relate to the Savings and Loan Industry* (Washington, D.C.: National Savings and Loan League, June 1974), pp. 54 ff. A further issue is the limit on accumulated loss reserves which is imposed on thrifts—the 6 percent fill-up.

industries since 1969 was predictable. But as time goes on and the level of the bad-debt allowance continues to decline, we would expect MSBs to take advantage of their portfolio powers to seek other routes of tax avoidance as alternates to residential mortgages. For example, since 1969, MSB holdings of municipals have increased nearly 400 percent, as compared to a 27 percent growth in holdings of residential mortgages, and an overall asset growth of 43 percent.[4]

Figure 2–2 shows the incidence of federal taxes, as reflected through (unadjusted) effective rates for commercial banks, S&Ls, and MSBs, by size of intermediary, for 1973. The line graphs show that the impact of federal tax increases with size of association for S&Ls but declines with increased commercial bank size. This reflects the limited ability of S&Ls to avoid federal tax beyond the bad-debt deduction allowance, a tax avoidance tool which is equally available to all associations, regardless of size. The pattern of taxation for commercial banks, on the other hand, is indicative of the economies of tax avoidance which exist for banks because of their wide and diverse investment powers. Leasing and foreign operations are primary methods through which banks are able to reduce their federal taxes, although the characteristics of these operations seem to lend themselves efficiently only to large-scale banking operations.[5]

The incidence of federal tax on mutual savings banks fluctuates by size-class, with a decline in tax impact in the largest bank classes (deposits of $500 million to $1 billion, and over $1 billion). There has been increased activity by MSBs in corporate and municipal securities since the 1969 Tax Reform Act, activities which in addition to intermediation in residential mortgages carry with them tax reduction consequences. Although further analysis with additional data sets is required, there is at least superficial evidence that, like large commercial banks, large MSBs are making use of their investment powers in order to aid in the reduction of their federal tax burdens.

The figures shown in the previous charts indicate that the impact of federal income taxes on commercial banks has been declining since about 1960, and that the federal tax burdens of S&Ls and MSBs have been increasing at various degrees and rates since 1962 as a consequence of the Revenue Act of 1962 and the Tax Reform Act of 1969. However, these effective rate measures

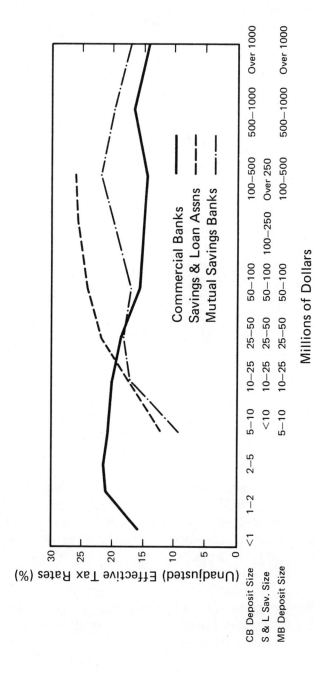

Figure 2–2. Unadjusted Effective Tax Rates for Major Depository Intermediaries, by Institution Size, 1973 (in Percentages)

(while useful in analyzing trends and relative changes in intra- and interindustry tax burdens over time) are not completely applicable to the primary issue of tax equity, or tax fairness, among competing institutions.

First, these measures ignore the costs of acquiring certain tax benefits. For example, interest paid on tax-exempt securities is below rates that are paid on taxable securities of comparable risk, such as U.S. governments. Consequently, only a portion of tax-exempt interest is a net addition to the economic income of the security holder. Effective rate calculations which ignore tax payments to foreign governments are biased downward when these rates are used for purposes of comparing relative tax burdens. On the other hand, economic income measures that recognize foreign tax payments must also recognize those subsidies that result from the U.S. tax treatment of foreign source income and taxes paid to foreign governments.[6]

More importantly, tax policy statements based upon the existing measure of effective tax rates ignore the impact of regulation on the economic income of an institution. In the case of financial institutions, regulations limit the types of assets, liabilities, or services that an intermediary may purchase or offer. For example, commercial banks presently are permitted to offer a wider variety of services than are either savings and loan associations or mutual savings banks. These powers represent a competitive advantage to commercial banks over the other two intermediaries, enabling banks to acquire customers (and thereby funds) through nonprice means. One can regard this as a net cost of regulation to S&Ls and MSBs. In essence, the question here is: What are the additional costs imposed on MSBs and S&Ls because they are not regulated in the same manner as commercial banks (as far as "full service" powers are concerned).[z] In this sense, the "full service" effect is an additional (regulatory) cost to S&Ls and MSBs in order to offset the benefit of these powers accruing to commercial banks. Assuming that the extent of this relative cost can be determined, estimates can then be provided as to the additional return on assets (or the increase in income) necessary in order to offset this cost of regulation. In assessing such matters as the relative tax treatment of different financial institutions, an (economic) income base used for

---

[z] This question, of course, applies as far as any regulatory differences are concerned.

comparative purposes should net out costs of regulation as an extraordinary expense as well as include any net benefits of regulation as an income item. As a further example of the kinds of imputations necessary in order to adjust for regulatory differences among commercial banks, S&Ls, and MSBs, the interest prohibition of demand deposits operates as a net benefit to commercial banks. It does so by permitting banks to raise funds at below market rates. Although banks do pay implicit rates on demand deposits by absorbing costs, evidence shows these to be below rates on time and savings accounts. Accordingly, S&Ls and MSBs must pay interest on all their deposits at rates comparable to those paid by banks on only part of their deposits; namely, savings deposits. The result is that a bank would receive a higher level of net income (or earnings on assets) than an S&L or MSB for any given level of gross income. On the other side of the coin, it can be argued that S&Ls benefit from differences in reserve requirements which exist between them and commercial banks. Commercial banks which are members of the Federal Reserve System are subject to reserve requirements on their deposits which are higher than those on S&Ls, and which require certain reserves to be held in a nonearning form. By comparison, S&Ls may fulfill their liquidity requirements by holding short-term government securities which pay interest. By tying up a portion of their assets in nonearning form, reserve requirements lower the rate of return on bank portfolios. Accordingly, this regulatory nuance shows up as a net benefit to S&Ls relative to commercial banks, requiring a greater return on a bank's portfolio in order to compensate for this regulatory constraint.[7] Reinforcing this reserve effect is the fact that S&Ls often have access to lower-cost borrowing facilities than do banks. Advances from the Federal Home Loan Bank System generally carry lower interest rates and longer terms than do comparable advances from the Federal Reserve System. The differential is compounded by the fact that commercial banks must often borrow through the Federal Funds market. Since Federal Funds rates are generally higher than the Federal Reserve discount rate, an additional cost is imposed on banks. There are, of course, other regulatory considerations when comparing these financial institutions, such as deposit insurance and branching restrictions. In addition, there are questions as to any benefits and costs accruing because of organizational form. Thus, mutuality permits funds to be raised at lower costs than by equity shares, a net benefit to federal S&Ls compared to stock forms. Limited evidence which is available indicates that bank holding companies, because of their organizational form, are more successful at reducing tax burdens than nonholding companies.

In the next chapter, we develop what we consider to be a more comprehensive economic income base upon which effective tax burdens of S&Ls can be determined, one that reflects certain regulatory considerations. By adjusting existing economic income measures in order to reflect costs and income-generating benefits imposed through regulation, the issue of tax equity through rate comparisons of competing intermediaries takes on a more meaningful interpretation.

3

The Income Effects of Regulation Within the Savings and Loan Industry

Introduction

The regulatory structure under which financial intermediaries operate influences the performance and the income-generating capacities of these intermediaries. Regulations restrict financial intermediaries largely by defining allowable asset holdings, fixing prices, or limiting spheres of operations. They impose a cost on an intermediary by forcing it to hold assets that it might not otherwise hold or forego the holding of assets it may wish to hold in the absence of regulations. Regulations also affect the operating income of intermediaries by forcing them into operations or pricing policies that would not be freely chosen. On the other hand, certain regulations generate benefits for intermediaries. To the extent that regulation stems from membership in the Federal Reserve System, Federal Home Loan Bank System, Federal Deposit Insurance Corporation, or Federal Savings and Loan Insurance Corporation, the regulated intermediary also receives services as part of that membership. As was stressed in the previous chapter, a measure of economic income should reflect costs and benefits of regulation in any discussion of tax equity among competing institutions. It is the purpose of this chapter to assay adjustments to the economic income of savings and loan associations which should be made because of certain regulations which affect these organizations.

There are two ways in which one can survey the costs and benefits of regulation. On the one hand, one may deal with the legal regulations which apply to all associations and estimate the net costs of these. Among these would be included regulations that bear on pricing and operating activities but only tangentially touch portfolios. On the other hand, one can look to the manner in which portfolios are affected by regulation, to the extent that they differ from what one might term an "ideal" portfolio.[a] This entails assessing the cumulative impact of regulation, in that portfolio com-

---

[a] "Ideal" here means the portfolio that would prudently be held in the absence of regulation.

position is a decision made over time and, to a great extent, reflects the longer-run forces governing the intermediary. We confine our investigation to the former approach.

In the first section of the chapter we consider the question of the implications of organizational form on the taxation of savings and loan associations. Presently, associations have the option of choosing to operate either as mutual or as stock organizations under either federal or state charter. If operating under mutual form, associations enter into ownership contracts with their depositors in that purchase of a deposit liability entitles the depositor to voting rights in the governance of organization. If operating as a stock company, purchase of a deposit secures no such rights. The organization is governed by owners of liability instruments other than deposits; namely, shares in the organization similar to shares in any other corporate enterprise.[b] This further implies that the profits generated by associations operating under different organizational forms are to be treated differently. Ideally, the payments made to owners in both cases are dividends and should be treated as such; additional interest paid by stock associations to depositors should be treated as business expense. These contentions flow naturally from the ruling principles of corporate tax treatment. However, this is not the way in which payments by different associations are treated. In fact, all payments made on deposits by savings and loan associations are treated as business expenses, and only dividend payments made by stock associations to holders of shares are treated as dividends in a manner similar to those of other corporations. This gives a de facto subsidy to mutual associations in that they may deduct payments made to owners, thus deducting payments for capital funds and lowering their net cost of capital. This subsidy, however, may be offset by the wider variety of variable rate capital instruments which stocks can offer, thus enabling them to raise capital more easily than mutuals, which can only offer a single type of deposit instrument subject to interest regulation. In addition, stocks are able to participate in holding company groups, giving them access to a wider variety of permissible assets and higher rates of return. If the tax laws affecting organizational forms for associations are to be neutral, the subsidy

---

[b] In reality, this ownership difference is somewhat obscure as mutual owners often sign away proxies to management. Yet the distinction remains in law and has implications for management strategy.

for mutuals should exactly balance off the advantages open to stocks, thus eliminating any incentive to operate under a specific form. However, it should be obvious upon reflection that since the advantages open to stock are not proscribed, and since the subsidy to mutuals depends crucially on the cost of alternative methods and costs of raising capital, the trade-off between these and the subsidy to mutuals cannot be of constant magnitude. The upshot of this is the fact that, at any given time, there will exist positive inducements for an association to operate as a mutual or as a stock.

In the following section we examine five basic regulations that impact S&Ls: the prohibition of the services that may be offered by savings and loans, the differential reserve requirements applicable to savings and loans, the interest rate differentials existing under Regulation Q, the prohibition of pledging of assets against public unit accounts, and the access to the lending facilities of the Federal Home Loan Bank System. In each of these, we first describe the nature of the regulation, then the costs and benefits generated by the regulation, and finally provide estimates as to those costs and benefits for all but the question of public unit accounts. We present these estimations both in terms of the additional earnings necessary on assets and in terms of the changes that would occur in operating income if the regulation were not present. In this manner, adjustments can be made to the economic income of associations in order to derive what we contend are more accurate measures of effective rates of federal taxation, both within the S&L industry and among competing intermediaries.

The Significance of Organizational Form for Savings and Loan Associations

At present, the large majority of savings and loan associations operate under the mutual form of organization. Of over four thousand insured associations, 85.4 percent operate under the mutual form.[c] In recent years, there has been a slight upward trend in stock intermediaries. In 1960, of 4,098 institutions, just under 13 percent were operating under stock form. These percentages, however, do not accurately reflect the relationship of stocks and

---

[c] 1974 figures.

mutuals in the savings and loan industry. Stock associations presently control almost 21 percent of all assets in the industry, an indication of their above-average size. This contrasts with the case in 1960 when stock associations, numbering 13 percent of the industry, controlled only 14.8 percent of its assets.

In terms of income, stock associations clearly dominate. With the exception of the smallest institutions (those with assets below $10 million), average income for stock associations is above that of mutuals. The greatest difference occurs in the largest sized institutions (those with assets over $250 million), where the average income for stock associations is half again as large as that of federal mutuals and nearly twice that of state mutuals. In fact, the difference grows as asset size increases. These figures are altered if we look at income net of operating expenses. Here the performance edge of stocks is even larger. For the largest associations, stocks have an average income nearly double that of federal mutuals and nearly triple that for state-chartered mutuals. Stock associations show higher income averages for all size classes of institution. This pattern of income is indicative of two characteristics exhibited by stocks. The first of these is a higher rate of return to the portfolio. This accounts for the gross income differential and, as expected, grows with institution size. The second characteristic is the greater efficiencies of stocks. Since regulatory and competitive considerations dictate that all associations must pay the same return to savings capital, net-income differences will diverge from gross-income differences only insofar as other operating expenses differ. Since the net-income edge of stocks over mutuals is greater than the gross-income edge, one must conclude that stocks sustain lower levels of operating expense than do mutuals. This can be a result of either implementation of modern operating techniques or more efficient use of borrowing outlets. In turn, both these characteristics reflect the age pattern of stocks and mutuals. The savings and loan industry has traditionally been a mutual industry, and thus the older associations operate under the mutual form. These have grown over time and reached some sort of steady state. Stock associations, on the other hand, are newer and tend to exhibit greater growth, thus accounting for the income flow variation.

This examination leads to another important comparison between stocks and mutuals; namely, the composition of the balance sheet. If the considerations stated are correct, one would expect to find stock companies holding a portfolio geared to growth assets relative to mutual holdings. A study by Donald Hester,[1] done for the Federal Home Loan Bank Board, dealt with this type of concern. Using the analysis of variance technique, Hester tested for regional and organizational form patterns with respect to portfolio composition, using federal mutuals as the benchmark. The data used were for the years 1960 and 1964. Hester found that stock associations generally held a significantly greater proportion of cash, non–U.S. government securities, share loans, and reacquired real estate assets than did mutual associations. In addition, stocks held a greater percentage of loans in process than mutuals. All these, with the possible exception of cash and security holdings, represent growth assets. Moreover, stocks were able to do this with a greater ratio of capital to assets, thereby indicating lower risk exposure. From this, Hester concluded that stock associations were quicker to utilize market opportunities efficiently as they arose.

An examination of several relevant balance sheet ratios of stocks and mutuals indicates that the trends cited by Hester remain at the present levels. The portfolios of stock associations seem to be geared more heavily toward growth assets than do the portfolios of mutuals. The ratio of reacquired real estate and contract loans is higher for stock associations than for either category of mutual. All this, of course, is modified by the fact that both forms of organization hold the vast majority of their portfolios in mortgage loans, and, when we speak of these trends, we are dealing with only a minor segment of the portfolio. However, the differences that these figures suggest are significant and must be considered.

As far as capital is concerned, large ($250 million and over) stock associations operate on a capital-asset ratio of 0.067, while large federal mutuals operate only on a ratio of 0.057 (1974 data). It thus appears that the Hester findings have held true to the present in that the largest class of stock associations is more aggressive with less risk exposure than the largest class of mutual associations.

Clearly, there are differences between the operations of mutuals and stock associations. Stocks appear to be more growth oriented and garner a much higher pretax net income than mutual associations even though they are only marginally larger in asset size. We can now examine the manner in which both forms of organization are taxed. As mentioned in the introduction to this chapter, there exists some conceptual basis for differentiating stocks and mutuals in terms of tax treatment; there also exists some practical basis for differential tax treatment in that the two portfolios differ. Table 3–1 indicates the rate of federal tax paid by size and type of association. On the basis of these exemplars, it seems that there is little difference in the rates paid by associations. Payment rates by mutuals are generally higher, but no sizable, consistent differences can be cited. This result is somewhat puzzling, since one would suspect that stock associations, with a more aggressive, growth-oriented asset policy would open themselves up to a higher level of taxation. Their high rate of current income and the progressive system seem to imply higher rates for stocks. That this is not so suggests the ability of stocks to take advantages of the tax system to a greater degree than mutuals.

Conventional economic theory deals with the firm strictly in the sense of a stock corporation. Management of the firm is assumed to be directed by owners to reach certain goals, usually assumed to be the maximization of profits. There are numerous problems with this basic approach when it comes to its applicability to modern corporations in general and savings and loan associations in particular. First, the question of the relevant goal for management does not have the clear-cut answer postulated by traditional theory. Several distinguished economists, notably William Baumol and J. K. Galbraith, have suggested that in the modern complex of oligopolized and monopolized industry, the

Table 3–1
Federal Tax Rates[a] for Savings and Loan Associations, by Asset Size and Organizational Form, 1973

Asset Size ($1,000,000)	(1) Federal Mutual (%)	(2) State Mutual (%)	(3) State Stock (%)
Under $10	12.5	14.0	11.3
$10–$25	18.3	18.5	17.2
$25–$50	22.5	22.5	22.5
$50–$100	24.6	25.4	23.5
$100–$250	26.1	25.4	24.7
Over $250	26.3	26.3	26.5

[a]Ratio of Federal taxes paid to taxable income plus excess bad-debt allowances.
Source: FHLBB, *Combined Financial Statements, 1973,* Washington, D.C.

corporation must pursue a goal of growth or sales maximization to insure its market position and thus its survival. These suggestions appear reasonable and serve to qualify traditional assumptions about the behavior of corporations. Secondly, the exact relationship between ownership and management in the modern corporation is in doubt. Traditional theory holds that owners dictate to managers with respect to objectives. In reality, management tends to exercise the proxies of owners in voting and, in effect, acts autonomously within certain limits. Clearly, exceptionally inept or criminal management or poor performance will generate ownership reaction and may cause the removal of management, but this direct intervention now occurs rarely. The tendency for management control of stock corporations is strengthened by the fact that managers are frequently stockholders as well and thus exercise partial ownership functions. Third, the theory of the firm says nothing about mutual organization. Given the original objectives of mutual firms, that is, temporary existence in order to fulfill a specific need and then dissolution, economic theory that is based on the immortality of corporate entities does not handle the form. While it may be reasonably argued that mutual organizations are no longer temporary, the problem yet remains that there is no definitive goal that may be imputed, and thus no clear-cut theory of mutual firms. Finally, the problem of diversification must be confronted. In the modern corporation, profit maximization may indeed be the goal, but this might imply a deliberate loss policy with respect to certain product lines of a multifaceted enterprise. Thus, we observe such phenomena as corporate control of professional sports teams which of themselves contribute losses but whose losses enable the parent group to reap tax advantages: the profitability of the entire enterprise is greater due to the losses of one unit. Traditional theory does not deal adequately with the multiproduct nature of the modern firm. For the savings and loan industry, this is especially crucial when treating the behavior of stock associations which participate in holding companies.

These thoughts suggest that there should be basic managerial strategies imputable to the firms that lie outside the realm of traditional theory. Since stock organizations are viewed as an investment by their owners, the stock manager is under pressure to perform. On the other hand, the mutual manager need only meet known contractual obligations to execute his assigned function. In the specific case of savings and loan associations, this distinction shows vividly. Both stock and mutual associations pay the same interest rate on their deposits, and both must maintain bad-debt reserves in the same ratio in order to remain viable. However, this comprises the entire goal of the mutual manager. If he earns enough from the association's portfolio to cover these commitments, he has fulfilled his function and additional surplus is a bonus to the owners of the mutual. On the other hand, the stock manager must generate an additional return (above interest and bad-debt reserve needs) from his portfolio in order to please the owners of the association. In addition, this surplus is subject to taxation, necessitating the stock manager to earn a higher pretax surplus in order to suit the posttax expectation of shareholders. All this suggests that the management of a stock association will be more aggressive than that of a mutual association in seeking out the highest yielding prudent asset.[2]

This aggressiveness seems to be confirmed by our earlier discussion in that stocks earn higher average levels of net and gross income than mutuals. It is confirmed in a more rigorous way in the work done by Kane and Valentini.[3] Using regression analysis, they find that stock-chartered associations, particularly those involved in holding companies, avail themselves of a much wider variety of tax deferral opportunities than do mutuals. One of the reasons cited for this fact is the more liberal state regulations under which most stock associations operate.[4] State regulations afford stock associations the option of holding a larger proportion of their assets in instruments independent of real estate. This portfolio diversification enables stocks to avoid taxes.

We have yet to explain, however, the pattern of rates paid by stocks and mutuals. If all the preceding is true, stocks should be paying lower rates than mutuals. Yet our data show that the two forms of organization pay at roughly comparable tax rates. The answer to this puzzle may lie in the fact that a firm operating under a mutual form of organization receives an implicit subsidy attached to that form.[d] The nature of this subsidy has been alluded to earlier, but it may be well to review it. Both stocks and mutuals must pay to raise funds with which they acquire assets. In the case of savings and loan associations, these payments are treated equally in taxa-

---

[d] This subsidy reduces costs and thus expands the income base on which our tax rates are calculated. This, in turn, lowers the effective rate paid by mutuals.

tion whether they arise out of the acceptance of deposits or the borrowing of funds through issuance of other debt. Both sets of payments are deductible from taxes, as cost of funds. Furthermore, additions to bad-debt reserves within legal guidelines may be deducted from taxable income. However, while these categories may exhaust the fund-raising methods used by mutuals, stock associations must make one more payment for funds; namely, dividends paid on capital stock. This represents an expense for funds which is not deductible from taxable income. To the extent that the costs of the mutual association in raising funds are wholly tax exempt while the costs for the stock associations are only partly so, a subsidy has been granted to mutual organizations.

It is possible to compute the degree of subsidy in a way that indicates its effect on the competitiveness of mutual vs. stock associations. We assume that, were they operating as stocks, mutuals would face the same cost of equity capital as stock associations.[5] Of this cost of equity, a portion is distributed to shareholders. The effective cost of capital for stock associations is thus the product of the cost of capital and the payout rate for dividends. This cost can be expressed as a function of total assets and operating income to give a complete picture of the additional return needed by stocks to cover their cost of capital; in other terms, the subsidy to the mutual association which raises all its capital in a tax-free manner. Thus, this subsidy should be added to the economic income of mutual associations for the purpose of estimating their true effective tax rate.

In the specific case of savings and loans treated here, we estimated the effective cost of capital for stocks to be the percentage of the profit rate paid out as dividends, reasoning that retained surplus serves the same function for both stocks and mutuals and thus does not represent an extraordinary cost for either. We then adjust this to get a pretax profit rate necessary to pay this additional cost. This is then translated into the additional rate of return which must be earned on assets and the corresponding operating income which would be necessary. These measure the subsidy to mutuals.

Table 3–2 presents the results of these estimations. Some interesting observations may be made in connection with these figures. First of all, the effective cost of capital for stocks is relatively invariant for different sized institutions, even though

Table 3–2
The Subsidy[a] to Mutuality[b] by Institution Size

	Asset Size in Millions of Dollars					
	Under $10	$10–25	$25–50	$50–100	$100–250	Over $250
(1) Profits/Net Worth	0.0554	0.0806	0.0905	0.0890	0.1041	0.1214
(2) Payout Rate	0.2452	0.2282	0.1655	0.1164	0.1286	0.1161
(3) Effective Cost of Capital [(1) × (2)]	0.0135	0.0183	0.0149	0.0103	0.0133	0.0140
(4) Additional Operating Profit Necessary [(3) ÷ (1 − tax rate)][c]	0.0151	0.0221	0.0189	0.0134	0.0174	0.0187
(5) Net Worth/Assets	0.0588	0.0638	0.0672	0.0627	0.0604	0.0583
(6) Assets/Operating Income	15.832	15.682	15.743	15.773	15.741	15.693
(7) Subsidy in terms of asset return [(4) × (5)]	0.0008	0.0014	0.0012	0.0008	0.0010	0.0010
(8) Subsidy in terms of Income [(6) × (7)]	0.0126	0.0219	0.0188	0.0126	0.0157	0.0157

[a]Explanations of these subsidies are found in the text.
[b]For federal mutuals only. Figures are similar, though slightly higher, for state mutuals.
[c]Tax rate derived from table 3–1, column 3.

profit rates show wide variance. The reason for this is that payout rates stand in an inverse relationship to profit rates. It thus appears that all stock associations pay the same rate of dividend, but whether this is coincidental or necessary for the attraction of sufficient capital, we cannot definitely say. It is a question that requires and merits further study. Secondly, the relationship of assets to operating income also appears relatively invariant with institution size. This is a bit more understandable, since we are dealing with an organization that specializes in mortgage lending so heavily that portfolios (and thus the earnings from them) will be similar for all sizes of institutions.

However, the most striking result of this calculation is the size of the mutual subsidy. What appeared to be a major difference between organizational forms turns out to be marginal at best. In terms of income, the subsidy is on the order of 1 to 2 percent. In other words, the reported income of mutuals needs to be adjusted upward by this percentage (due to the mutual form of organization) in order to reflect the adjustment in economic income for this organizational form of associations. Alternatively, mutual portfolios are subsidized in an amount in the neighborhood of ten basis points (0.1 percent). This means that, all else being equal, stocks must earn this much more on their portfolios in order to be competitive with mutuals. In neither case does the implicit subsidy due to tax considerations appear to be something that presents any real barriers to competition among the two.

In terms of effective tax rates, the subsidy is also marginal. If we adjust economic income levels (as defined in chapter 2) for the subsidy, we may derive new adjusted, comparative tax rates for insured S&Ls. This is a more accurate rate since it corrects for an implicit subsidy of the tax-regulatory system. Table 3–3 displays these results. Clearly, while the mutual subsidy lowers effective rates for mutual institutions, the difference is negligible, amounting to no more than 0.4 percent for any institution size. This contrasts vividly to the estimates presented by the American Bankers Association.[6] Their figures calculate the tax effects at 7.1 to 8.7 percent for the period 1966–69, with a long-run average of 13 percent. While this includes an adjustment for holdings of municipal securities[e] and is based on data for years prior to our data, the

---

[e] Since holdings of municipals by savings and loans are small, this should be negligible.

Table 3–3

Federal Tax Rates[a] of Savings and Loan Associations, Adjusted for Mutuality Subsidy, by Asset Size, 1973

Asset Size ($1,000,000)	Without Adjustment (%)	Adjusted for Mutuality (%)
Under $10	13.0	12.8
$10–$25	18.2	17.8
$25–$50	22.5	22.2
$50–$100	24.7	24.4
$100–$250	25.7	25.3
Over $250	26.3	25.9

[a]See Table 3–1.
Source: Tables 3–1 and 3–2.

discrepancy is alarming in view of the fact that the same basic method of calculation is used. We can attribute the difference to two facts. First of all, the ABA calculations assumed an identical cost of share capital between banks and savings and loan associations. As has been pointed out, the cost of capital to banks is much higher—nearly double that of savings and loan associations. Secondly, the amount of share capital which would have to be raised by savings and loan associations in the absence of the mutual "subsidy" is estimated on the basis of commercial bank experience. Since commercial banks savings deposits represent a much smaller percentage of bank liabilities than do similar deposits for savings and loans, using bank experience increases the estimated value of share capital needed by savings and loans in the absence of mutuality. Both these factors bias upward estimations of the implicit tax subsidy to mutual organizations and should account for the discrepancy between our figures and those of the ABA.[f]

---

[f] Kane, who may or may not represent some sort of dominant view on this issue, discusses the ABA calculations and concludes that no mutuality adjustment should be made at all in deriving comparative economic income bases. He states that:

> Such calculations as this one [ABA adjustment for mutuality] give economics a bad name. Neither the method of allocating bank dividends, the naive extrapolation of bank dividend rates to mutuals, nor the use of a 40 percent tax rate is microeconomically sound. Approaching the problem from the point of view of a mutual shareholder, for the years since 1966 the proper adjustment for mutuality is essentially zero. One should be able to establish that matched pairs of stock and mutual thrift institutions pay essentially the same rates to savers, all the more so in the years since the Interest Rate Control Act. There is no market for the so-called ownership element in mutual "shares" nor do these shares provide legally enforceable rights to the institution's net assets. In instances where state-chartered mutuals have converted to stock charters, court-approved proce-

Regulatory Costs and Benefits Impacting the Savings and Loan Industry

Prohibition of Services and Regulation Q Differentials

At present, savings and loan associations are restricted from offering many of the services that make commercial banks "full service" institutions. These services include safe-deposit facilities, credit cards, and a full range of lending activity. This credit extension ability provides a strong attraction for depositors, since deposits with the commercial bank may be evidence of creditworthiness for loan purposes. In order to offset this attraction, savings and loan associations must offer higher dividends on their own deposit accounts. This deposit premium acts as a price inducement to overcome the service advantage of commercial banks. However, payment of this premium will raise the level of operating costs and thus reduce the net income of savings and loan associations. Hence, the prohibition of services imposes a cost on the regulated association. We may estimate this cost in a relatively straightforward manner. First, a deposit premium must be assigned to commercial bank services. Available estimates place this premium in the range of 0.53 to 0.83 percent (53 to 83 basis points).[7] Lapidus[8] notes that these estimates tend toward the high side and suggests 50 basis points as reasonable in view of the fact that commercial bank offices are more numerous than savings and loan offices and this tends to obscure the necessary premium. We assume 50 basis points as the deposit premium necessary on savings and loan deposits to offset commercial bank services. Second, we translate this into asset and operating income effects. To do so, we calculate the ratio of savings deposits to total assets and multiply this by our deposit premium to establish the additional earnings

dures for dividing the surplus among shareholders have ignored the pattern of shareholders' investment and disinvestment during the time the surplus was accured, treating these distributions as lottery-windfalls to be prorated arbitrarily as of a single day's deposits. Proposed rules are under consideration by the FHLBB to govern conversions of federally-insured SLAs to stock charters. These rules, which prorate accumulated surpluses on the basis of a forward-looking weighted average of each customer's deposit holdings, continue to ignore the claims of past shareholders to earning accumulated with funds they supplied.

See Edward J. Kane, "Federal Income-Tax Burdens of Commercial Banks and Savings and Loan Associations," p. 13.

rate necessary on assets to offset this premium. To arrive at the necessary increase in operating income, we multiply the additional earnings rate by the ratio of assets to operating income. These calculations are presented by size of institution in table 3–4.

The prohibition of services is a significant cost of regulation to savings and loans, with the actual cost in the 6 to 7 percent range for operating income, and in the area of 43 basis points on added return on assets. What this means is that, *all else being equal*, savings and loans must earn 0.43 percent more on assets, or generate 6.5 percent more income from assets, than commercial banks in order to overcome the full service powers of banks. This result does not differ substantially among different sized institutions. To translate these effects into effective tax rates, we treat the prohibition against full-service accounts as a cost of business and adjust economic income accordingly. The results are shown in table 3–5. The prohibition of services raises the effective tax rate for associations on average by 1.5 to 2.0 percentage points.

Some qualifications must be added to this, however, and they deal largely with the effects of Regulation Q. Since 1966, thrift institutions have been subjected to the same type of interest rate controls as commercial banks. However, as an aid to the housing market, the actual ceiling rate payable on deposits has remained higher for thrifts than for banks. Between 1966 and the beginning of

Table 3–4
Effect of Prohibition of Services on Savings and Loans, by Institution Size

Asset Size ($1,000,000)	(1) Savings Deposits Total Assets	(2) Savings Deposits Operating Income	(3) Asset Effect $(1) \times \left(\dfrac{Deposit}{Premium}\right)^a$	(4) Income Effect[b] (2) × (3)
Under $10	0.885	14.079	0.0044	0.0703
$10–$25	0.874	13.755	0.0043	0.0687
$25–$50	0.864	13.596	0.0043	0.0679
$50–$100	0.858	13.483	0.0043	0.0674
$100–$250	0.849	13.340	0.0042	0.0667
Over $250	0.836	12.889	0.0042	0.0644

[a]This represents percentage point increase in return necessary for S&Ls to remain competitive with full service institutions in the attraction of deposits; deposit premium assumed to be 0.5 percent.

[b]This represents percentage point increase in income which must be generated by S&Ls to maintain a competitive position.

Source: FHLBB, *FSLIC-Insured S&LA's Combined Financial Statements.*

Table 3–5
Effect of Prohibition of Services on Effective Tax Rates of Savings and Loan Associations, by Size Class, 1973

Asset Size ($1,000,000)	Effective Tax Rate Exclusive of Effect of Prohibition (%)	Effective Tax Rate Including Prohibition (%)
Under $10	13.0	14.2
$10–$25	18.2	19.5
$25–$50	22.5	24.3
$50–$100	24.7	26.9
$100–$250	25.7	27.6
Over $250	26.3	28.1

Source: Table 3–3 and FHLBB, *FSLIC-Insured S&LA's Combined Financial Statements*, 1973.

1970, the interest ceiling differential was in the 0.75 to 1.0 percent range. This would, according to our previous line of reasoning, more than adequately allow thrifts to offset full-service banking. Thus, for this period, the calculations in table 3–4 represent a close approximation to the cost of this regulation of service provision. Since 1970, however, the ceiling differential for thrifts has been reduced to 0.25 percent on passbook accounts. It would seem that this reduction places thrifts at an additional disadvantage since it restricts the deposit premium they can employ to attract deposits. If this were the case, then the true cost of service prohibition for thrifts would be higher than our calculations indicate. Unfortunately, there is little empirical evidence to justify this contention, and one limited study[9] has shown that the competitive position of thrifts (based on analysis of deposit flows) has improved in this period. We simply present these considerations and conclude that an interest rate differential of 0.5 percent is neutral in that it favors neither thrifts nor banks. This differential is necessary if excess burden imposed on thrifts is to be avoided, given existing regulatory limitations. Consequently, our estimations of table 3–4 stand as the estimated cost of service regulation on savings and loan associations.

Reserve Requirements

Presently, savings and loan associations operate under a lower set of liquidity requirements than do commercial banks. Federal Reserve member banks[g] must hold up to 13.5 percent reserves against demand deposits and up to 6 percent reserves against time deposits. These reserves must be held in nonearning form, either in cash or in deposits with the Federal Reserve. On the other hand, savings and loan associations need only hold 5.0 percent of their portfolio in reserves,[h] and this may be held in the form of interest-bearing, short-term obligations. The fact that savings and loans can conduct an intermediary function with control of a greater portion of their portfolio than their competitors represents a subsidy to these institutions.[i]

We can calculate the size of this subsidy in the following manner. First of all, we estimate the effective reserve requirement on commercial banks by dividing total required reserves by total deposits. We then subtract from this the ratio of cash to total assets for savings and loans to arrive at a figure representing the percentage of the portfolio that must be transferred from interest-earning to non-interest-earning form if savings and loans were to be regulated as commercial banks. Next, we adjust this by the percentage of savings deposits to assets and generate operating income and asset effects. These latter adjustments are done by assuming that reserves are to be created through transfers from all assets proportionately, so the net effect on the portfolio is to reduce the return by the average portfolio return adjusted for the percentage of earning assets.[j] The results of these calculations are presented in table 3–6.

Note that the degree of the subsidy given to savings and loan associations by reserve requirements is very similar to the costs imposed by the service prohibitions. Our estimates for this subsidy range from 41 to 51 basis points on assets and 6.3 to 8.0 percent of operating income. This means that savings and loans, *all else being*

---

[g] In order to simplify matters, we deal here only with FRS and FHLBB members, the bulk of institutions. The reader is warned that figures do not apply to state-regulated institutions.

[h] The reserve requirement at the time of this writing.

[i] To be completely accurate, we should include the return available to non-FRS member commercial banks through the lodgement of reserves with their correspondent institutions. We do not do so here, since we are confining ourselves to the sterile deposits of member banks. Gatti, ''Expanded Deposit Powers,'' makes such a calculation.

[j] This is slightly unrealistic, as lowest yield assets would be the first to be liquidated, but is a necessary simplification for the analysis. This overstates the size of the imputed benefits to S&Ls.

Table 3–6
Effect of Differential Reserve Requirements on Savings and Loan Associations, by Institution Size
(Commercial Bank reserve requirement = 7.8 percent)

Asset Size ($1,000,000)	(1) Cash / Deposits	(2) Savings Deposits / Assets	(3) Return on Assets	(4) Earning Assets / Total Assets	(5) Assets / Operating Income	(6) Asset Effect[a]	(7) Operating Income Effect[a]
Under $10	0.00122	0.885	0.0628	0.989	15.906	0.0043	0.0683
$10–$25	0.00106	0.874	0.0637	0.987	15.732	0.0043	0.0676
$25–$50	0.00098	0.864	0.0635	0.986	15.765	0.0042	0.0662
$50–$100	0.00096	0.858	0.0636	0.986	15.713	0.0042	0.0659
$100–$250	0.00095	0.849	0.0782	0.986	15.718	0.0051	0.0801
Over $250	0.00108	0.836	0.0648	0.999	15.413	0.0041	0.0631

[a]Effects are as defined in table 3–4, except that now they represent reduction of return or income which savings and loan associations could absorb with no change in competitive position.

Source: See table 3–4.

Table 3–7
Effect of Differential Reserve Requirement on Effective Tax Rates of Savings and Loan Associations, by Size Class, 1973

Asset Size ($1,000,000)	Effective Tax Rate Exclusive of Reserve Subsidy (%)	Effective Tax Rate Including Reserve Subsidy (%)
Under $10	13.0	12.3
$10–$25	18.2	17.1
$25–$50	22.5	21.2
$50–$100	24.7	23.3
$100–$250	25.7	24.0
Over $250	26.3	25.7

Source: See table 3–5.

equal, can earn about 0.5 percent lower returns on assets and still remain competitive with commercial banks, due to lower reserve requirements. Thus, the difference in reserve requirements lends a subsidy to savings and loans associations in the range of 6 to 8 percent of operating income, an income adjustment that must be added to existing measures of economic income in order to arrive at a more complete and accurate calculation of effective rates of taxation. When this is done, the effective rates for savings and loan associations are lowered (see table 3–7).

Access to Lending

Members of the Federal Home Loan Bank System are able to borrow from the system at rates that are in fact below the market. This differential allows savings and loan associations to support a given portfolio at a cost lower than would otherwise be possible. This ability to borrow represents a net benefit of regulation.[k]

This subsidy can be calculated in the following manner. First, the difference between the rate on FHLBB advances and a market rate is calculated. It is clear that this result will be biased by the specific rate chosen, so we opt for a long-term rate since this best reflects both the nature of savings and loan borrowing needs and the nature of FHLBB advances. The rate chosen is an average of

---

[k] Again, we omit non-FHLBB members.

highest grade corporate and utility bonds. Next, we calculate the ratio of FHLBB advances to total assets and multiply this by our interest rate difference to arrive at an asset effect, then multiply that by the ratio of assets to operating income in order to determine an operating income effect. Table 3–8 presents these results.

The advantages flowing to savings and loan associations from access to FHLBB advances are minimal, amounting to at most 5 basis points on assets and three-quarters of 1 percent on operating income. For the sake of completeness, we include this subsidy element in economic income of associations while at the same time noting its relative insignificance.[1] Table 3–9 displays the tax consequences of the borrowing privilege. It is, as expected, small, amounting to only one-tenth of a percentage point on average.

The Holding of Public Unit Accounts

The passage of H.R. 11221 by the Congress brings to the fore the relationship between public unit deposits and private depository intermediaries. The bill raises insurance limits on deposits on in-

Table 3–8
Effect of Access to FHLBB Advances,
by Institution Size
(Average FHLBB Advance Rate = 6.00 percent)
(Average Long-term Bond Rate[a] *= 7.26 percent)*

Asset Size ($1,000,000)	(1) Advances Total Assets	(2) Assets Operating Income	(3) Asset Effect	(4) Income Effect (2) × (3)
Under $10	0.0178	15.906	0.0002	0.0031
$10–$25	0.0232	15.732	0.0002	0.0031
$25–$50	0.0256	15.765	0.0003	0.0047
$50–$100	0.0265	15.713	0.0003	0.0047
$100–$250	0.0329	15.718	0.0004	0.0062
Over $250	0.0435	15.413	0.0005	0.0077

[a]Rate is average of Aaa utility and corporate bond rates.

Sources: S&L data—see table 3–4; Long-term bond rate: *Federal Reserve Bulletin*, December 1973, p. A34.

---

[1] It should be noted that this calculation shows the subsidy in its greatest magnitude, since we have chosen one of the highest market interest rates as our comparison base.

Table 3–9

Effect of Borrowing Privilege on Effective Tax Rates of Savings and Loan Associations, by Size Class, 1973

Asset Size ($1,000,000)	Effective Tax Rate Exclusive of Borrowing Privilege (%)	Effective Tax Rate Including Privilege (%)
Under $10	13.0	12.9
$10–$25	18.2	18.1
$25–$50	22.5	22.4
$50–$100	24.7	24.6
$100–$250	25.7	25.5
Over $250	26.3	26.1

Source: See tables 3–5 and 3–8.

sured institutions. Specifically, it raises the insurance limit on private accounts from $20,000 to $40,000 per account, and to $100,000 on time and savings deposit accounts of public units; that is, federal, state, and local governmental divisions. Such an increase in insurance would have little effect on actual coverage, as the present limit fully insures over 98 percent of all accounts (with 60.9 percent of all deposits, as of mid-1975). The increased limit would cover an additional 1 percent of all accounts and 9 percent of deposits. This is a somewhat marginal change, as it leaves the level of insurance coverage virtually unchanged. The increase in the limit may reduce costs to account holders in that the effort expended in maintaining two or three separate accounts in order to fully insure deposits can now be saved by the individual account holder. While one might infer this result on the basis of theory, it is not quantifiable.

As of the end of June 1975, government units held a little over $70 billion in deposits at insured commercial banks. Of these, the majority were held by nonfederal units and were held in time deposits ($48.2 billion). These represent the entirety of public deposits in the financial system, due to the pledging requirement. This requirement, enforced by the federal government and 38 states, forces financial institutions holding public deposits to pledge certain classes of assets as collateral against these deposits. The amount of the pledge varies, but usually ranges from 100 percent to 120 percent of the amount on deposit. In states where the pledging requirement does not hold full force, some partial pledging is required. By regulation, federal savings and loan associations are precluded from pledging assets. In lieu of pledged assets, most jurisdictions will accept deposit insurance, so that savings and loan associations can accept public deposits up to the insurance limit. However, although this limit is $100,000, public unit deposits come in much larger amounts, and S&Ls are effectively shut out of the market for public deposits.

The pledging requirement also affects financial markets. Generally, pledged assets are required to be securities of the depositing governmental unit, be it state, local, or federal. The result is that the pledging situation serves as a prop to the market for certain securities, mainly state and local issues. By requiring pledging, public units increase the demand for their securities, raising their price, lowering interest rates, and thus reducing the cost of raising funds. Hence, the relationship between public units and commercial banks works to the benefit of both parties, on the one hand reducing borrowing costs and on the other hand giving banks a steady flow of funds.

Numerous studies have appeared in economic literature[10] showing that the pledging association has a significant effect on the asset acquisition strategy of commercial banks. The most salient study in the area, done by Charles Haywood in 1967,[11] found that a vast majority of asset decisions are influenced by the pledging requirement. Subsequent studies have shown that pledging requirements significantly (in a statistical sense) affect the demand by commercial banks for state and local securities. Such a relationship is readily understandable, as the pledge requires that state and local securities be held. Since, as Haywood found, public unit deposits are generally more volatile than other deposits, banks will in fact overpledge; that is, pledge more than the required ratio of assets.

However, this requirement is not the burden it appears to be. Commercial banks are naturally attracted to municipals, regardless of pledging requirements. The interest from municipals is tax exempt: this is available to all taxpayers. However, intermediaries are unique in their ability to claim a (de facto) tax deduction for the interest paid on funds raised in order to purchase the municipals. This double tax break for commercial banks has produced an upsurge in bank holdings of municipal bonds. Between 1966 and 1974, commercial banks acquired nearly 65 percent of all municipals issued, well in excess of the municipals necessary to meet pledging requirements. These considerations tend to support the claim by some that the pledging requirement represents but a minor reason for the purchase of state and local obligations by commercial banks.

Thrift institutions have been, as pointed out earlier, effectively precluded from holding public unit deposits by both regulatory and insurance limitations. This is partially responsible for the low percentage of municipal obligations in the portfolios of thrift institutions. The restriction stems from the belief that the short-term nature of public unit deposits and the securities that are pledged against them work against the fundamental mission of thrift institutions to promote housing finance. However, there is a stronger reason for the disassociation of thrift institutions from public unit deposits; namely, the fact that, unlike banks, the pledging requirement would impose a true burden on thrifts. Up until recently, the holdings of municipals which necessarily accompany public unit deposits do not offer the tax savings available from mortgage holdings. The current bad-debt allowance, usable by thrifts holding mortgages, provides a lower level of taxation than would the tax-free income from municipals. However, with the declining bad-debt allowance as mandated under the Tax Reform Act of 1969, the holdings of municipals are becoming more attractive to thrift institutions. Under these circumstances, it is understandable that thrifts are now more interested in obtaining public unit deposits, the flow of funds they represent, and the municipal holdings they require.

With respect to the deposit-holding public, public unit accounts have two distinct implications. In the first case, they increase the risk exposure of those accounts of greater than $40,000 (the insurance limit). This is due to the fact that pledging on public unit accounts gives to governmental units preferential claim on the assets of an insolvent institution. Hence, in cases of insolvencies, account holders will be unable to recover a pro rata share of bank assets. Second, the tying up of funds in short-term securities, which is inherent in pledging, alters the volume of loans supplied by banks and makes those loans more costly than they would be without pledging. H.R. 11221 opens the public unit deposit market to thrift institutions by partially insuring these deposits, thus circumventing the pledging requirement. This entrée for thrifts is by no means an undiluted blessing or curse either to public units, thrifts, or banks, and the issues involved need to be defined.

The major contention of the thrift industry is that the complete insurance of public unit deposits will aid the housing market by generating a new flow of funds into thrift institutions. This increase in funds flow will work in the long run to reduce interest rates on mortgages. The criticisms of this position are many. They revolve around the supposed volatility of public unit funds. John Petersen of the Municipal Finance Officers Association[12] contends that public unit accounts are basically short-term funds that are placed in short-term instruments, notably certificates of deposit. In this case, these funds cannot be allocated to long-term use, that is, housing loans, since they show little stability. This contention is countered by the fact that well over 65 percent of all public unit funds are placed in time deposits, a notably more stable form of deposit.

It is unclear what impact public unit account holdings by thrifts would have on the cyclical nature of the housing market. If these deposits are as subject to disintermediation as private deposits, they will flow out in periods of high interest rates and flow in when interest rates fall, thus intensifying housing cycles. On the other hand, since funds are placed in public unit accounts in anticipation of expenditure, there is reason to believe that these deposits are less interest sensitive than private deposits. If this is the case, and if high interest rates (and thus disintermediation) are associated with rising incomes, tax receipts will rise and more public funds will flow into thrift institutions. This will ease the upward pressure on mortgage interest rates and compensate for some of the adverse effects of disintermediation. This argument suggests that the extension of public unit account power to savings and loan associations will have a moderating effect on housing cycles. In either case, it is instructive to note that savings and loan associations have successfully integrated public funds in tax escrow accounts into their asset portfolios, with little, if any, adverse experience.

A final criticism of the insurance proposal that would, de facto, allow thrifts to hold public unit deposits is that it would severely damage the market for municipal securities. As funds shift from commercial banks to thrifts, pledged assets will no longer be held and the market for government obligations, supported so strongly by commercial banks, will become thinner. If this is the case, borrowing costs will rise for state and local units. Petersen, citing a study by George Petersen and Harvey Galper,[13] claims that a permanent reduction in bank demand for municipals of $3 billion would drive up municipal bond rates by 0.6 percent, and would thus increase the interest cost of borrowing by some $300 million per year for these governmental units. There is no reason to doubt this claim; however, as pointed out previously, pledging is but one reason for the acquisition of government obligations by banks. The clear tax advantage inherent in these instruments and the availability of these securities for year-end tax switching purposes lead us to believe that the full insurance of public unit deposits, while it might cause these deposits to flow into thrifts, will be unlikely to cause any drastic alteration of the municipal bond market. This conclusion is strengthened by the belief cited earlier that a declining bad-debt allowance will induce thrifts to make more frequent use of this market, thus adding to its strength.

Summary

Tables 3–10 to 3–13 present a summary of our estimates of the comparative costs of regulation to depository intermediaries as expressed through changes in their effective tax rates. Table 3–10 shows these results for savings and loan associations based on

Table 3–10
Impact of Implicit Taxes and Subsidies on Effective Federal Tax Rates of Savings and Loan Associations, by Size Class, 1973[a]
(In Percentage Points)

Asset Size ($ million)	Prohibition of Services	Reserve Structure	Borrowing Privilege	Effect of Mutual Form of Organization	Total Impact[a]
Under $10	+1.2	−0.7	−0.1	−0.2	+0.2
$10–$25	+1.3	−1.1	−0.1	−0.4	−0.3
$25–$50	+1.8	−1.3	−0.1	−0.3	+0.1
$50–$100	+2.2	−1.4	−0.1	−0.3	+0.4
$100–$250	+1.9	−1.7	−0.2	−0.4	−0.4
Over $250	+1.8	−0.6	−0.2	−0.4	+0.6

[a]Total impact is the sum of the first four columns. One would adjust effective rates by adding these figures to the unadjusted rates.
Source: Tables 3–4 to 3–9.

Table 3-11
Impact of Regulation on the Effective Federal Tax Rates of Mutual Savings Banks, by Size Class, 1973
(*In Percentage Points*)

Asset Size ($ million)	Differential Reserve Requirements[a,b]	Prohibition of Services[a]	Access to Borrowing[a]	Form of Organization[a,c]	Total[d]
Under $10	(−0.19)–(−0.41)	+0.51	+0.02	(−0.18)–(−0.22)	(−0.10)–(+0.16)
$10–$25	(−0.35)–(−0.78)	+0.93	+0.02	(−0.44)–(−0.46)	(−0.29)–(+0.16)
$25–$50	(−0.36)–(−0.79)	+1.38	+0.03	(−0.35)–(−0.64)	(−0.02)–(+0.70)
$50–$100	(−0.33)–(−0.72)	+1.27	+0.03	(−0.22)–(−0.59)	(−0.01)–(+0.76)
$100–$500	(−0.45)–(−0.98)	+1.22	+0.03	(−0.28)–(−0.89)	(−0.62)–(+0.52)
$500–$1000	(−0.41)–(−0.88)	+1.03	+0.03	(−0.22)–(−0.81)	(−0.58)–(+0.48)
Over $1000	(−0.36)–(−0.76)	+0.98	+0.03	(−0.19)–(−0.70)	(−0.45)–(+0.46)

[a]Positive entry indicates regulatory cost; negative entry indicates regulatory subsidy. See Biederman and Tuccillo, *Taxation and Regulation of MSBs*, for discussion of regulatory items.

[b]Given as a range due to alternative commercial bank reserve requirement assumptions. See Biederman and Tuccillo, *Taxation and Regulation of MSBs*, pp. 27 ff.

[c]Given as range due to alternative stock organization assumptions. See Biederman and Tuccillo, *Taxation and Regulation of MSBs*, pp. 42–50.

[d]Sum of previous four columns. One would adjust effective rates by adding these figures to the unadjusted rates.

Source: Kenneth R. Biederman and John A. Tuccillo, *The Taxation and Regulation of Mutual Savings Banks* (Washington, D.C.: National Savings and Loan League), 1975, tables II–6, II–8, II–10, II–12, II–14.

Table 3–12

Impact of Regulation on Effective Federal Tax Rates of Commercial Banks, by Size Class, 1973

(In Percentage Points)

Asset Size ($ million)	Interest Prohibition[a,b] on Demand Deposits	Borrowing Privileges[b]	Total[c]
Under $1	−1.81	0.00	−1.81
$1–$2	−1.81	−0.02	−1.83
$2–$5	−1.81	−0.02	−1.83
$5–$10	−1.81	−0.01	−1.82
$10–$25	−1.81	−0.02	−1.83
$25–$50	−1.81	−0.03	−1.84
$50–$100	−1.77	−0.04	−1.81
$100–$500	−1.66	−0.11	−1.77
$500–$1000	−1.66	−0.21	−1.87
Over $1000	−1.66	−0.31	−1.97

[a]Averaged over following asset classes, $0–50 million; $50–100 million; over $100 million.

[b]See Biederman and Tuccillo, *Taxation and Regulation of Commercial Banks* for discussion of regulatory items.

[c]Sum of previous two columns. One would adjust effective rates by adding these figures to unadjusted rates.

Source: Kenneth R. Biederman and John A. Tuccillo, *The Taxation and Regulation of Commercial Banks* (Washington, D.C.: National Savings and Loan League), 1974, table II-8, p. 103.

those regulations as discussed in previous sections of this chapter. Tables 3–11 and 3–12 present analogous results for mutual savings banks and commercial banks. Although not explicitly derived in this text, the methodology employed is essentially the same as that used in the regulatory analysis for savings and loan associations.[14] Table 3–13 summarizes all of this by showing, by institution size, effective federal tax rates for the three major depository intermediaries. The rates shown are for 1973, calculated using the traditional concept of economic income for these organizations, and recalculated to indicate the impact of the relative costs and benefits of regulation on these rate calculations.[m]

An accounting of the implicit (comparative) benefits and costs

[m] The reader will recall that the analysis of the impact of regulation on the economic income of S&Ls was conducted by treating each regulation as a regulatory cost, or benefit, relative to commercial banks. Thus, to recalculate the impact of the cost, or benefits, of the same regulation on the effective rates of commercial banks would be double counting the relative cost or benefit of that regulation. Accordingly, the only regulatory entries shown in table 3–11 for commercial banks are those that were not germane in the analysis of regulation affecting S&Ls.

Table 3–13
Unadjusted and Adjusted Effective Tax Rates for Major Depository Intermediaries, by Institution Size, 1973
(In Percentages)

Asset Size — Insured Mutual Savings and Insured Commercial Banks ($1,000,000)	Asset Size — Insured Savings & Loans ($1,000,000)	Insured Commercial Banks		Insured Savings & Loan Associations		Insured Mutual Savings Banks	
		Unadjusted[a]	Adjusted[b]	Unadjusted[a]	Adjusted[b]	Unadjusted[a]	Adjusted[b]
Less than $1		15.8	14.0				
$1–2		22.8	21.0				
$2–5		22.9	21.1				
$5–10	Less than $10	21.7	19.9	13.0	13.2	9.7	9.6– 9.9[c]
$10–25	$10–25	20.4	18.6	18.2	17.9	18.0	17.7–18.2
$25–50	$25–50	18.6	16.8	22.5	22.6	18.3	18.2–18.9
$50–100	$50–100	15.5	13.8	24.7	25.1	16.6	16.6–17.3
	$100–250			25.7	25.3		
$100–500	More than $250	14.5	12.7	26.3	26.9	22.4	21.8–22.9
$500–1000		16.4	14.5			19.8	19.2–20.3
More than $1000		14.2	12.2			17.0	16.5–17.5

[a]Effective rate using definition for economic income as employed in Treasury Department, *Tax Reform Studies and Proposals*. Essentially this amounts to taxable income plus (1) bad-debt deductions in excess of experience; (2) tax-exempt interest; (3) net operating loss carry-overs; and (4) 85 percent of domestic dividends received. Consequently, these figures have not been adjusted in order to reflect regulatory differences.

[b]Effective rates adjusted for regulatory effects.

[c]See Biederman and Tucillo, *Taxation and Regulation of Mutual Savings Banks*, p. 50, for explanation of range of adjusted tax rates.

Source: FDIC, *Annual Report*, 1973; FHLBB, *Combined Financial Statements*, 1973; tables III-10 and III-11.

of regulation as reported in table 3–13 shows that these regulatory differences: (1) exacerbate the current tax inequities that exist between S&Ls and commercial banks; (2) improve the competitive position of banks vis-à-vis MSBs to the point where the regulation-taxation burden of mutual savings banks equals, or in certain instances exceeds, that of commercial banks; (3) leaves the competitive differences that exist between MSBs and S&Ls under the present tax system relatively unchanged.

There are two specific implications of this analysis for public policy. First of all, the regulatory system, weighing more heavily as it does on the major housing lenders in the economy, has a dampening impact on the housing market. To the extent that the power of thrifts to compete with commercial banks for funds is constrained, the flow of funds into housing is diminished.

Secondly, and related to this, the evidence presented here bears upon the impact of the current proposals for reform of the financial sector. The Financial Institutions Act, currently being considered by the Congress, would remove much of the differential impact of the regulatory system by extending the powers of thrifts. An analysis of the provisions of this bill conducted for HUD[15] indicates that this extension of powers would enable thrifts to compete more strongly for funds and would increase the flow of funds into housing.

The Financial Institutions Act includes specific provisions for changes in the tax treatment of financial intermediaries. Thus, the proposed legislation presents an integrated package of tax and regulatory reform which appears, at least on the surface, to recognize the existence of tax and subsidy elements in the regulation of competing depository intermediaries. In the next chapter, we analyze these proposed changes in the tax treatment of savings and loan associations.

4 The Mortgage Tax Credit

Introduction

In the previous chapters, we have seen evidence of a rapidly changing federal tax picture impacting savings and loan associations. We have shown that the reasons for this are the institution of the minimum tax and major changes in the structure of the bad-debt deduction allowances. In light of changing regulatory structures facing financial institutions, it has been widely suggested by sources both in and out of the thrift industry[a] that the federal tax treatment of thrift institutions be altered. Among tax reformers, there is little sympathy for the continuation of the bad-debt reserve deduction.

The most oft-cited alternative to the bad-debt deduction is the mortgage tax credit, which was mentioned in the Hunt Commission Report and which was part of the Financial Institutions Act of 1975.

Title VII of the Financial Institutions Act eliminates the percentage-of-taxable-income method of calculating loss reserves for thrift institutions. Under this proposal, further reserve additions on qualifying loans would be computed under either the percentage-of-eligible-loan or the experience methods presently available to commercial banks. In lieu of the bad-debt reserve allowance, Title VII proposes a tax credit be granted equal to a specified percentage of gross interest income from qualifying residential mortgages. A qualifying residential mortgage loan is further defined in the proposed legislation as an agreement that constitutes a first lien against real property, provided such property is located in the United States or a possession thereof, and is either: (1) a loan secured by an interest in real property which is or will become residential—therefore, covering home improvement loans, single- or multi-family dwellings, mobile homes not used on a transient

---

[a] The Hunt Commission, the Financial Institutions Acts of 1973 and 1975, the FINE Commission, the American Bankers Association, the Treasury, and the Federal Reserve Board, just to name a few.

65

basis, and facilities in residential developments; or (2) a loan secured by interest in real property located within an urban renewal area to be developed for predominately residential use (under an approved urban renewal plan) or located within a so-called model cities area.

In the case of the mixed-use dwellings, the whole loan is deemed to be qualifying if planned residential use exceeds 80 percent of total planned development use. Loans made to finance development or acquisition would also qualify, if there is "reasonable assurance" that the property would become residential real property within a period of three years. The credit cannot exceed the tax imposed less the sum of other tax credits allowable, but a credit "carry-back" of three taxable years and a "carry-forward" of seven years is provided.

For individual taxpayers (including partners, beneficiaries of estates and trusts, and Subchapter S shareholders), the credit would be equal to 1.5 percent of the qualifying residential mortgage interest income earned during the taxable year. For other taxpayers, the credit would vary, depending on the level of investment in residential mortgages. If at least 70 percent of the taxpayer's assets are in qualifying residential mortgage loans, the credit would be equal to 3.5 percent of gross interest income. The tax credit percentage would be reduced by one-thirtieth of 1 percent for each one percentage point qualified assets falling below 70 percent in any taxable year. If less than 10 percent of assets are in qualifying residential mortgage loans, the taxpayer would be ineligible for the mortgage interest tax credit.[b]

In the 1975 version of the Financial Institutions Act (FIA), a thrift institution could continue to be taxed under the provisions of the current bad-debt allowance, if it so chooses, until 1979. After that time, the mortgage tax credit would apply to all savings and loans and mutual savings banks. Prior to 1980, an election by a thrift to use the mortgage tax credit in any given year would be irrevocable, and accordingly the tax credit would then apply to all subsequent years.

---

[b] The Financial Institutions Act as reported out of the Senate Committee on Banking, Housing, and Urban Affairs as S. 1267 modifies this tax provision from the administration proposal by allowing a tax credit of 3-5/6 percent for institutions holding 80 percent of their assets in qualifying residential mortgages. The phase-out provisions are the same, with a floor of 10 percent in order for an institution to qualify for the mortgage tax credit.

In this chapter, we look at the concept of a neutral mortgage tax credit for alternative levels of the bad-debt allowance (BDA), projecting the total tax performance of the industry over the next five years under the proposed tax credit. To provide a direct comparison, we then look at alternative tax rates for savings and loan associations under both the bad-debt allowance and the mortgage tax credit with various assumptions as to asset growth and net income behavior. Finally, we investigate, on a preliminary basis, the adequacy of the proposed mortgage tax credit from the standpoint of promoting funds flows into housing.

The "Neutral" Mortgage Tax Credit for S&Ls

For thrifts, the bad-debt deduction is based upon net, or taxable, income whereas the proposed mortgage tax credit would be dependent upon certain "qualified" gross income. Thus, any comparisons made between these two tax systems would be sensitive to assumptions concerning both the absolute and relative levels of the two income concepts.

One way of looking at the notion of a compensating (or neutral) mortgage tax credit in comparison with the bad-debt allowance is by employing the analytical technique which we used in our treatment of the minimum tax.[c] Basically, the intent of this analysis is to determine the size of the (mortgage) tax credit that would be necessary in order to offset the loss of a given percentage bad-debt deduction for *an asset that would qualify for either tax privilege* (such as a residential mortgage). For these purposes, it is assumed that all conditions of qualification have been met by an association so that the maximum amount that can be claimed for tax purposes under both the bad-debt allowance and the mortgage tax credit are in fact claimed.

In order to develop the algorithm relating the mortgage tax credit to the bad-debt deduction, we introduce the following notation:

$\bar{X}$ = an asset that would fully qualify for both the bad-debt allowance provisions and the mortgage tax credit

---

[c] See Chapter 2, *The Minimum Tax*.

X' = gross income originating from $\bar{X}$

X = before-tax income (net income before the bad-debt deduction) originating from $\bar{X}$

X'' = aftertax income before the mortgage tax credit is claimed, originating from $\bar{X}$

$X''\,'$ = aftertax income after the mortgage tax credit is claimed, originating from $\bar{X}$

BDA = bad-debt deduction (expressed as a percentage; e.g., in 1976, BDA = 0.43)

MTC = mortgage tax credit (expressed as a percentage; e.g., MTC = 0.035 is the administration's proposed mortgage tax credit ceiling)

Employing these symbols, *the aftertax income originating from a qualifying asset ($\bar{X}$) under the provisions of the bad-debt allowance* would be given by the expression:

$$X'' = X - [(X - (BDA)X)\,(0.48)] -$$
$$0.1\,[(BDA)X - 0.48\,(X - (BDA)X)] \qquad (4.1)$$

The second expression on the right side represents regular taxes which would be paid under a given bad-debt allowance; that is, before-tax income (X) less the permitted bad-debt deduction (BDA) (X), times the marginal tax rate (0.48).

The third expression in equation 4.1 represents the minimum tax that would be imposed on income that is not subject to the regular income tax because of the bad-debt deduction.[d] The minimum tax would be 10% (= 0.01) of the bad-debt deduction $[(BDA)X]$ less regular taxes paid $[0.48(X - (BDA)X)]$. Since both of the bracketed expressions are federal taxes paid on income originating from $\bar{X}$, before-tax income must be reduced by both expressions in order to arrive at aftertax income (X''). *Under the bad debt deduction*

$$X'' = X''\,' \qquad (4.2)$$

inasmuch as mortgage tax credit provisions are not applicable.

---

[d] For these calculations, it has been assumed that the $30,000 exemption from the minimum tax has already been taken.

As an example, assume that BDA = 0.40; i.e., the permitted bad-debt deduction equals 40 percent of before-tax income.[e] Accordingly:

$$X'' = X - [(X - 0.4X)\ (0.48)] - 0.1[(0.4)X - 0.48(X - 0.4X)];$$
$$\text{or } X'' = 0.7008X \qquad (4.2a)$$

This can be interpreted that under a bad-debt allowance of 40 percent of net income and the current minimum tax, the aftertax return on a qualified asset (X) will be slightly more than 70 percent of its before-tax return.[f]

Turning now to the mortgage tax credit, *the aftertax, before the mortgage tax credit, income originating from an asset that qualifies for the mortgage tax credit* would be given by:

$$X'' = X - 0.48X = 0.52X \qquad (4.3)$$

Notice that in equation 4.3 there is no allowance for the bad-debt deduction, nor is there any mention of the minimum tax. This is a reflection of the fact that under the FIA proposals, neither of these provisions would be connected with the mortgage tax credit plan.

In order to incorporate the mortgage tax credit into equation 4.3, it is necessary to establish the ratio between gross income originating and net income originating from $\bar{X}$; i.e., essentially account for cost of funds associated with the acquisition of $\bar{X}$. Thus, if we let $(N)\ (X) = X'$, where X' and X are as previously defined, and N is a pure number establishing the relationship of X' to X, the expression for income originating from $\bar{X}$ after tax and after the mortgage tax credit can be written:

$$X'' \,' = 0.52X + (\text{MTC})\ (NX) \qquad (4.4)$$

Since our notion of a "neutral" mortgage tax credit is one that would leave aftertax, after-credit income the same as under the bad-debt deduction, setting equation 4.4 equal to equation 4.1 will yield this "neutral" mortgage tax credit for any given level of BDA, and for any ratio of net (before tax) income to gross income on the qualified asset:

---

[e] This will be the allowance in 1979 and thereafter.

[f] "Before-tax return" is taxable income plus the bad-debt allowance.

$$0.52X + (MTC)\ (NX) = X - [(X - (BDA)X)\ (0.48) - 0.1$$
$$[(BDA)X - 0.48(X - (BDA)X)]\quad (4.5)$$

As an example, let BDA = 0.4 as in the previous example, and assume that $N = 5$.[g]

Given these values, equation 4.5 is written:

$$0.52X + (MTC)\ (5X) = X - [(X - 0.4X)$$
$$(0.48)] - 0.1[(0.4X) - 0.48(X - 0.4X)];$$
$$\text{or MTC} = \frac{0.1808X}{5X} = 0.0362 \quad\quad (4.5a)$$

Thus, a mortgage tax credit of 3.62 percent would be needed in order to compensate for the loss of the bad-debt allowance under the assumptions of a bad-debt allowance at the 1979 level and a gross-net income ratio of 5. Table 4–1 shows similar results from the algorithm in expression (5) for various levels of BDA and N.

These results, based on a marginal analysis, are consistent with our findings in a study in which we conducted a similar analysis based on aggregated data sources.[1] They show that in what would be regarded as good and exceptional years in terms of net return ($N = 5.56$ and $N = 5.0$ respectively), a mortgage tax credit in excess of 3.5 percent would have been necessary in order to compensate for the loss of the bad-debt deduction. This conclusion does not hold up, however, for years of low return ($N \times 6.67$ and $N \times 8.33$), nor does it hold up beyond 1975 for any except very high return situations ($N = 5$). Based upon what could reasonably be expected to be average performance levels, a mortgage tax credit in the range of 2.8 to 3.2 percent would compensate for loss of the bad-debt allowance for most associations for most years after 1978.

One of the ways Congress may very well reduce the value of the bad-debt deduction would be through the minimum tax. During the last congressional go-around on this matter, the two changes that were more frequently proposed were the elimination of the deduction for regular taxes paid and the doubling of the minimum tax rate from 10 to 20 percent. We can incorporate these potential changes in the minimum tax into the algorithm derived in expres-

[g] Recent experience has shown that this would represent an exceptionally good year in terms of net before-tax return for most associations. In 1973, the all-industry average was $N = 5.72$, and was 8.02 in 1974.

Table 4–1
Neutral Mortgage Tax Credit[a] Under Alternative Bad-Debt Deduction Allowances and Different Ratios of Gross to (Before-Tax) Net Income[b]

	Neutral Mortgage Tax Credit			
BDA	N = 5.00	N = 5.56	N = 6.67	N = 8.33
0.60 (1969 level)	4.95%	4.44%	3.70%	2.97%
0.45 (1975 level)	3.95	3.55	2.96	2.37
0.42 (1977 level)	3.76	3.38	2.82	2.25
0.40 (1979 level & thereafter)	3.62	3.25	2.71	2.17

[a]Neutral mortgage tax credit defined as the tax credit which should be necessary in order to compensate for loss of the bad-debt deduction under stated assumptions.

[b]Marginal tax rate = 0.48; current minimum tax assumed. All symbols as previously defined.

sion (5) in order to test the sensitivity of the "neutral" mortgage tax credit to such alterations. In the first set of simulations, the deduction for regular taxes paid, which is presently allowed under the minimum tax, is eliminated. Accordingly, equation 4.5 is rewritten:

$$0.52X + (MTC)(NX) = X - [(X - (BDA)X)(0.48)] - 0.1[(BDA)X]^h \tag{4.6}$$

Using equation 4.6, a sensitivity analysis similar to that shown in table 4–1 was conducted. These results are presented in table 4–2. The results of an analysis similar to that behind the findings in tables 4–1 and 4–2 are shown in table 4–3. In table 4–3, the current minimum tax is altered by doubling the minimum tax rate. Accordingly, equation 4.5 is now rewritten:

$$0.52X + (MTC)(NX) \times X - [(X - (BDA)X)$$
$$(0.48)] - 0.2[(BDA)X -$$
$$0.48(X - (BDA)X]^i \tag{4.7}$$

A comparison of tables 4–1 to 4–3 indicates the degree to which these changes in the minimum tax would alter the size of the

[h] All symbols as defined previously.

[i] All symbols as defined previously.

Table 4–2

Neutral Mortgage Tax Credit Under Alternative Bad-Debt Deduction Allowances and Different Ratios of Gross to (Before-Tax) Net Income; Variation I on the Minimum Tax[a]

	Neutral Mortgage Tax Credit			
BDA	N = 5.00	N = 5.56	N = 6.67	N = 8.33
0.60 (1969 level)	4.56%	4.10%	3.42%	2.74%
0.45 (1975 level)	3.42	3.08	2.56	2.05
0.42 (1977 level)	3.20	2.88	2.40	1.92
0.40 (1979 level & thereafter)	3.04	2.73	2.28	1.82

[a]Current minimum tax without deduction for regular taxes paid. See table 4–1 for identification of symbols.

mortgage tax credit necessary for offsetting the loss of the bad-debt allowance, under the assumption set chosen. As evidenced in these tables, changes in the minimum tax would further reduce the attractiveness of the current bad-debt provision to the point where a mortgage tax credit in the range of 2.2 to 3.0 percent, *or lower*, would compensate for the elimination of the bad-debt allowance in terms of industry tax reduction.

Tax Performance Projections—Mortgage Tax Credit

In a previous section, we pointed out that over the full phase-in period of the Tax Reform Act of 1969, the tax rate of savings and loan associations would rise considerably. This rise is caused by a declining bad-debt allowance, the minimum tax, and (possibly) the 6 percent fill-up limitation of the bad-debt allowance. Depending on asset growth rates and income assumptions, this tax rate increase ranges from 6 to 10 percentage points relative to 1973 levels.

The situation with respect to the mortgage tax credit is somewhat different. Since the rate of the credit is not variable and there is no limitation (such as the 6 percent fill-up clause), there would be (other things equal) no progression over time in the tax rate that would be paid by associations under the mortgage tax credits. However, the rate is significantly affected with respect to the relationship of net income to gross income originating from qualified assets, as indicated in the previous section. Table 4–4 reflects

Table 4–3
Neutral Mortgage Tax Credit Under Alternative Bad-Debt Deduction Allowances and Different Ratios of Gross to (Before-Tax) Net Income; Variation II on the Minimum Tax[a]

	Neutral Mortgage Tax Credit			
BDA	N = 5.00	N = 5.56	N = 6.67	N = 8.33
0.60 (1969 level)	4.13%	3.71%	3.09%	2.48%
0.45 (1975 level)	3.58	3.22	2.68	2.15
0.42 (1977 level)	3.47	3.12	2.60	2.08
0.40 (1979 level & thereafter)	3.39	3.05	2.54	2.04

[a]Current minimum tax with rate doubled to 20 percent. See table 4–1 for identification of symbols.

Table 4–4
Tax Performance of Savings and Loan Associations Under 3.5 Percent Mortgage Tax Credit, by Size of Association, 1975 and 1979

	1975		1979	
Asset Size ($ millions)	Tax Rate— High Income[a] (percentage)	Tax Rate— Low Income[b] (percentage)	Tax Rate— High Income[a] (percentage)	Tax Rate— Low Income[b] (percentage)
I. Five Percent Asset Growth[c]				
Less than 10	30.5	13.0	30.5	13.0
10–25	30.5	13.0	30.5	13.0
25–50	30.5	13.0	30.5	13.0
50–100	30.5	13.0	30.5	13.0
100–250	30.5	13.0	30.5	13.0
More than 250	30.5	13.0	30.5	13.0
II. Historical Asset Growth[d]				
Less than 10	30.5	13.0	30.5	13.0
10–25	30.5	13.0	30.5	13.0
25–50	30.5	13.0	30.5	13.0
50–100	30.5	13.0	30.5	13.0
100–250	30.5	13.0	30.5	13.0
More than 250	30.5	13.0	30.5	13.0

[a]Ratio of gross to net income equals 5. Tax rate calculated as a percentage of net income.
[b]Ratio of gross to net income equals 10. Tax rate calculated as a percentage of net income.
[c]Assumption is that qualified assets grow at 5 percent annual rate.
[d]Assumption is that qualified assets grow at their 1969–73 average annual rate.
Source: FHLBB, Random sample of 1,000 association balance sheets and income statements, 1973 data base.

this sensitivity by showing tax rates that would be paid by associations under the mortgage tax credit proposal for extreme levels of gross-net return. Our data come from the sample of 1,000 individual associations mentioned previously. We project tax rates using these data as a base under certain assumptions as to asset growth rates, portfolio return rates, and ratios of net-to-gross income. Our asset growth rate assumptions are identical to those used for the bad-debt allowance analysis in chapter II. We assume a gross portfolio return of 7 percent, a figure that appears, in light of current yields on mortgages, to be representative of average gross yields on qualified assets in the near future. Our "high" income assumption utilizes a payout rate of 80 percent (that is, one-fifth of gross return remains after expenses, including interest payments), while our "low" income projection assumes a payout rate of 90 percent.[j] The results in table 4–4 deserve some comment.

First of all, tax rates under the mortgage tax credit are invariant with respect to asset growth rates or association size[k] because tax bills under the mortgage tax credit were calculated with reference to percentages of assets and the rate of income from those assets. Thus, no matter what the absolute size or growth rate of the association, the tax rate is constant. What differs is the tax bill. For the low-income example cited, at the 5 percent asset growth rate, average tax bills in 1979 would range from $5,800 for the smallest class of associations to $479,000 for the largest class of associations. Secondly, the tax rate paid by associations under the mortgage tax credit is sensitive to the ratio of net-to-gross income. Partially this is technical, partially it is a reflection of the tax system. The technical reason is that tax rates are calculated with reference to a credit based on gross income. The other reason is the procyclical nature of the tax credit. If interest rates rise, gross income should rise as well (due to the addition of higher-yield, net assets), but so should interest expenses as deposit rates rise to meet the market.

---

[j] Two points need be made here. First, our 20-percent figure represents an extreme which associations have not approached recently and thus must be regarded as a maximum. Secondly, these ratios should not be confused with those symbolized in an earlier section by the letter "N." The present ratio compares net income to total gross income, while "N" compares net income to only the gross income originating from qualified (for the mortgage tax credit) assets. Accordingly, for a given level of "N" as defined previously, this ratio would be greater.

[k] We are ignoring the $25,000 exemption from the 26-percent corporate surcharge. To that extent, rates for the smaller associations are overstated.

Since asset returns are on the average (long run) but interest-dividend costs on the margin (short run), the ratio of gross-to-net income rises. Of course, during a period of falling rates, the opposite occurs. An example may help:

1. Let A stand for net income and B stand for gross income from qualified assets.

2. Assume that $(N')(A) = B$, and the mortgage tax credit is 3.5 percent.

Then, for any gross income,

Tax credit $= 0.035\ B$

and

Taxes payable $= 0.48\ A - 0.035\ B$

Substituting:

Taxes payable $= 0.48A - 0.035\ (B)\ (A) = (0.48 - 0.035\ N')\ (A)$

and

$$\text{Tax rate} = [(0.48 - 0.035N')A]/A, \qquad\qquad (4.8)$$

since tax rates are conventionally defined in terms of net income. Clearly, the larger is N', the smaller is the tax rate. This is precisely what is shown in our tables: the tax rate falls from 30.5 percent to 13 percent as the ratio of gross to net income (N') rises from 5 to 10. The upshot of all this is that the exact tax pattern for savings and loan associations under the mortgage tax credit proposal is not readily identifiable, but rather depends upon the portfolio return, net of nontax expense. If recent historical experience is any guide, the ratio of gross to net income (N') will fall close to 6.67.[1] Substituting this into our previous example gives a long-run tax rate of 24.7 percent, which is lower than that which would result under the bad-debt allowance.[m] This is consistent with our findings as reported in table 4–1.

---

[1] Recent trends in interest rates and deposit flows indicate that a figure *no greater than* 15 percent would be applicable here.

[m] See table 4–6.

Table 4–5

A Comparison of Average Tax Bills and Tax Rates for Savings and Loan Associations under the Bad-Debt Allowance (Full Phase-In) and the Proposed Mortgage Tax Credit, by Asset Size of Association, 1979 Levels

(Average Return on Portfolio = 7 Percent)

Asset Size Class ($ millions)	(Below-Average Growth in Assets— High Rate of Net Return)			
	Average Tax Bill—Bad-Debt Allowance (BDA) ($000)	Average Tax Bill— Mortgage Tax Credit (3-1/2%) ($000)	Tax Rate— Bad-Debt Allowance (BDA) (percentage)	Tax Rate— Mortgage Tax Credit (3-1/2%) (percentage)
Less than 10	19.5	16.4	29.2%	24.7%
10–25	54.1	45.8	29.1	24.7
25–50	117.0	98.3	29.4	24.7
50–100	223.7	189.8	29.1	24.7
100–250	485.2	408.9	29.3	24.7
More than 250	1592.0	1363.5	28.8	24.7

Notes: 1. These are projections based on the assumption of continued activities similar to current portfolio structure.

2. No allowances made for first $25,000 exemption from 26 percent corporate surcharge; therefore, all rates on small associations marginally overstated.

3. Figures do not show minimum tax. Add about 10 percent to *Tax Bill* under BDA and 10 to 12 percent to *Tax Rates* under BDA to reflect effect of minimum tax.

Source: FHLBB, Random sample of 1,000 association balance sheets and income statements, 1973 data base.

An Aggregate Comparison of the Mortgage Tax Credit and the Bad-Debt Allowance

To get a better feel for the relationship of these two tax structures, we can examine directly five-year projections of tax rates under the bad-debt allowance and mortgage tax credit. Tables 4–5 to 4–8 present these rates and tax bills for the beginning and end years of this period, 1975 and 1979, subject to certain assumptions as to asset growth rates and net returns. Specifically, we use a 5 percent annual asset growth to represent below-average growth in assets and the 1972–73 rate of 12 percent to represent an above-average growth rate in assets. Our high rate of net return assumes a net-to-gross income ratio of 15 percent, while our low rate of net return

Table 4–6

A Comparison of Average Tax Bills and Tax Rates for Savings and Loan Associations under the Bad-Debt Allowance (Full Phase-In) and the Proposed Mortgage Tax Credit, by Asset Size of Association, 1979 Levels

Asset Size Class ($ millions)	*Average Tax Bill—Bad-Debt Allowance (BDA) ($000)*	*Average Tax Bill— Mortgage Tax Credit (3-1/2%) ($000)*	*Tax Rate— Bad-Debt Allowance (BDA) (percentage)*	*Tax Rate— Mortgage Tax Credit (3-1/2%) (percentage)*
Less than 10	12.5	5.8	29.0%	13.0%
10–25	35.6	16.1	28.8	13.0
25–50	76.5	34.5	28.8	13.0
50–100	147.7	66.7	28.8	13.0
100–250	318.3	143.7	28.8	13.0
More than 250	1061.3	479.0	28.8	13.0

(Below-Average Growth in Assets— Low Rate of Net Return)

Notes:
1. These are projections based on the assumption of continued activities similar to current portfolio structure.
2. No allowances made for first $25,000 exemption from 26 percent corporate surcharge; therefore, all rates on small associations marginally overstated.
3. Figures do not show minimum tax. Add about 10 percent to *Tax Bill* under BDA and 10 to 12 percent to *Tax Rates* under BDA to reflect effect of minimum tax.

Source: FHLBB, Random sample of 1,000 association balance sheets and income statements, 1973 data base.

uses a 10 percent ratio.[n] Throughout these simulations, we use a gross rate of return to assets of 7 percent, which we feel best represents the long-term return to current portfolios. Tables 4–5 to 4–8 present a number of alternative scenarios in that they show various combinations of asset growth rates and net income performance. As an example, table 4–6, which shows tax rates and average tax bills generated by below-average growth in assets and low rate of net return, could depict a year such as 1974, where high market interest rates generated both disintermediation and increased interest payment expenses. Table 4–7 represents a good year, such as 1973, where savings inflows were strong and net returns high. Thus, these tables represent some alternative futures.

[n] Again, this differs from the ''N'' ratio used earlier; rather it is equal to N' referred to in footnote j. The actual industry performance has ranged between $N' = 10\%$ and $N' = 15\%$.

Table 4–7

A Comparison of Average Tax Bills and Tax Rates for Savings and Loan Associations under the Bad-Debt Allowance (Full Phase-In) and the Proposed Mortgage Tax Credit, by Asset Size of Association, 1979 Levels

	(Above-Average Growth in Assets— High Rate of Net Return)			
Asset Size Class ($ millions)	Average Tax Bill—Bad-Debt Allowance (BDA) ($000)	Average Tax Bill— Mortgage Tax Credit (3-1/2%) ($000)	Tax Rate— Bad-Debt Allowance (BDA) (percentage)	Tax Rate— Mortgage Tax Credit (3-1/2%) (percentage)
Less than 10	21.6	18.5	28.8%	24.7%
10–25	71.3	60.8	28.8	24.7
25–50	155.0	132.8	28.8	24.7
50–100	307.3	263.8	28.8	24.7
100–250	656.4	562.2	28.8	24.7
More than 250	2237.3	1916.6	28.8	24.7

Notes: 1. These are projections based on the assumption of continued activities similar to current portfolio structure.
2. No allowances made for first $25,000 exemption from 26 percent corporate surcharge; therefore, all rates on small associations marginally overstated.
3. Figures do not show minimum tax. Add about 10 percent to *Tax Bill* under BDA and 10 to 12 percent to *Tax Rates* under BDA to reflect effect of minimum tax.

Source: FHLBB, Random sample of 1,000 association balance sheets and income statements, 1973 data base.

It must be remembered that no single one of these tables will show exactly what the performance of the industry will be over the next five years; the truth will lie in some combination of these four scenarios. The value of this exercise is to point out the sensitivity of the two tax structures to changing economic conditions in the savings and loan industry.

On the basis of these figures, several comments are in order:

1. They quantify our earlier notion that the tax rate resulting from the mortgage tax credit structure is highly sensitive to the ratio of net-to-gross income. As this ratio is varied from the high rate of 15 percent to the low rate of 10 percent, effective tax rates drop from 24.7 percent to 13.0 percent.

2. Under the bad-debt allowance, slow rates of asset growth make the 6 percent fill-up clause operative much quicker. This in turn results in marginally higher effective tax rates.

Table 4–8

A Comparison of Average Tax Bills and Tax Rates for Savings and Loan Associations under the Bad-Debt Allowance (Full Phase-In) and the Proposed Mortgage Tax Credit, by Asset Size of Association, 1979 Levels

	(Above-Average Growth in Assets— Low Rate of Net Return)			
Asset Size Class ($ millions)	*Average Tax Bill—Bad-Debt Allowance (BDA) ($000)*	*Average Tax Bill— Mortgage Tax Credit (3-1/2%) ($000)*	*Tax Rate— Bad-Debt Allowance (BDA) (percentage)*	*Tax Rate— Mortgage Tax Credit (3-1/2%) (percentage)*
Less than 10	14.4	6.5	28.8%	13.0%
10–25	47.3	21.3	28.8	13.0
25–50	103.3	46.6	28.8	13.0
50–100	204.9	92.5	28.8	13.0
100–250	437.6	197.5	28.8	13.0
More than 250	1491.9	673.4	28.8	13.0

Notes: 1. These are projections based on the assumption of continued activities similar to current portfolio structure.
2. No allowances made for first $25,000 exemption from 26 percent corporate surcharge; therefore, all rates on small associations marginally overstated.
3. Figures do not show minimum tax. Add about 10 percent to *Tax Bill* under BDA and 10 to 12 percent to *Tax Rates* under BDA to reflect effect of minimum tax.

Source: FHLBB, Random sample of 1,000 association balance sheets and income statements, 1973 data base.

3. The mortgage tax credit becomes much more desirable in periods of below-average growth in assets and low rates of net return. There are several reasons for this. First, tax rates under the mortgage tax credit are lower with low rates of net return. Secondly, tax rates under the bad-debt allowance are higher when asset growth is slower. Third, high gross rates of return are associated with low net rates of return, making a tax reduction based on a gross return, such as the mortgage tax credit, much more attractive.

4. The relative attractiveness of the mortgage tax credit is, of course, a function of the size of the credit.

Table 4–9 reproduces the tax rates and average tax bills of table 4–5, but assumes a 5 percent credit. Clearly, the higher credit with its resulting lower tax rate would result in much greater tax savings for the savings and loan industry.

Table 4–9

A Comparison of Average Tax Bills and Tax Rates for Savings and Loan Associations under the Bad-Debt Allowance (Full Phase-In) and a 5 Percent Mortgage Tax Credit, by Asset Size of Association, 1979 Levels

	(Below-Average Growth in Assets— High Rate of Net Return)			
Asset Size Class ($ millions)	*Average Tax Bill—Bad-Debt Allowance (BDA) ($000)*	*Average Tax Bill— Mortgage Tax Credit (5.0%) ($000)*	*Tax Rate— Bad-Debt Allowance (BDA) (percentage)*	*Tax Rate— Mortgage Tax Credit (5.0%) (percentage)*
Less than 10	19.5	9.8	29.2%	14.7%
10–25	54.1	27.3	29.1	14.7
25–50	117.0	58.5	29.4	14.7
50–100	223.7	113.0	29.1	14.7
100–250	485.2	243.4	29.3	14.7
More than 250	1592.0	811.5	28.8	14.7

Notes: 1. These are projections based on the assumption of continued activities similar to current portfolio structure.

2. No allowances made for first $25,000 exemption from 26 percent corporate surcharge; therefore, all rates on small associations marginally overstated.

3. Figures do not show minimum tax. Add about 10 percent to *Tax Bill* under BDA and 10 to 12 percent to *Tax Rates* under BDA to reflect effect of minimum tax.

aSource: FHLBB, Random sample of 1,000 association balance sheets and income statements, 1973 data base.

5. None of these calculations include minimum tax considerations. At present, it is not clear whether the minimum tax would still apply if the bad-debt allowance were replaced by the mortgage tax credit—we feel that this would not be the case. In any event, the tax rates under the bad-debt allowance are understated by some 2 to 3 percentage points because of this omission.

6. Should the actual level of the tax credit vary, the trade-off between the mortgage tax credit and the bad-debt allowance would also change. To get some idea of the sensitivity of tax rates to the size of the credit, we calculated tax rates using the high rate of net return and a 7 percent gross return together with the 1973 portfolio structure, but varied the size of the credit. These results are displayed in table 4–10. Clearly, as the size of the credit falls, tax rates rise by greater and greater amounts.

Table 4–10
A Comparison of Effective Tax Rates for the Savings and Loan Industry under Alternate Levels of Mortgage Tax Credit[a]

Mortgage Tax Credit	Effective Tax Rate
3.5%	24.7%
4.2	19.9
4.6	17.3
5.0	14.7
5.3	12.7

[a]Assumptions:
1. Average return on assets equals 7%.
2. High rate of net return (marginally better net return than 1972–73 performance levels).
3. Portfolio structure as in 1973.

7. Following upon this and noting the graduated nature of the MTC, it appears that this tax measure would tend to equalize the tax burdens of thrifts and commercial banks. While the MTC will reduce taxes for all intermediaries, the heavier investment in mortgages by thrifts means that their tax burdens would be reduced more than that of banks, which invest less heavily in qualifying mortgages. Based on our previous observations as to the relative tax burdens of intermediaries, this is an equity-inducing move.

The trade-off between the bad-debt allowance and the mortgage tax credit with respect to tax savings for savings and loan associations is clear, and summarized in the preceding tables. Given the current state of the economy, high mortgage interest rates, and recurrent credit crunches (involving disintermediation), our projections clearly indicate that the 3.5 (maximum) percent mortgage tax credit generates greater benefits for the savings and loan industry than the existing bad-debt allowance. Even under a favorable scenario of high growth rates and net returns, these figures show that, by decade's end, the savings and loan industry would enjoy the greatest amount of tax saving under the mortgage tax credit scheme.

The Mortgage Tax Credit: An Adequate Subsidy?

In addition to stating that the mortgage tax credit will "place competing institutions on an equal tax footing," the Treasury promises that the mortgage interest tax subsidy will assure a steady flow of funds into housing. We have examined the equity issue at length, exploring the question of tax equity among competing financial institutions under the present federal tax structure as well as examining the prospects under the proposed revision. Setting the equity debate aside for the moment, in this final section we approach the question as to whether the proposed 3.5 percent mortgage tax credit would indeed be adequate from the standpoint of housing flows.

One way to look at this issue is by viewing the mortgage tax credit in terms of its effect on rates of return. The mortgage tax credit can be translated into an interest-equivalent subsidy; that is, into an increase in gross return necessary to generate the same aftertax return without the tax credit, by means of the following algorithm. Let $\bar{i}$ be the gross rate of return on a portfolio that qualifies for the full 3.5 percent mortgage tax credit. Alternatively, let $\bar{r}$ be the gross rate of return on a nonqualifying portfolio. If we let i equal the before-tax return from $\bar{i}$, and r the before-tax return originating from $\bar{r}$, then $0.52i$ and $0.52r$ would represent their aftertax returns, respectively.[o] But, $0.52i$ is not the net, aftertax return originating from $\bar{i}$, since an allowance must now be made for the mortgage tax credit. Letting i' equal the net, aftertax return originating from $\bar{i}$, and r equal the aftertax return originating from $\bar{r}$, then

$$i' = 0.52i + 0.035\bar{i};\text{[p]} \text{ and} \qquad (4.9)$$

$$r' = 0.52r \qquad (4.10)$$

Equality of the aftertax returns on the two portfolios implies:

$$0.52i = 0.035\bar{i} = 0.52r \qquad (4.11)$$

If the nonqualifying portfolio is going to earn the same rate of return as the qualifying one, then obviously $r > i$; or,

$$r = i + X \text{ where } X > 0. \qquad (4.12)$$

---

[o] Forty-eight percent tax rate. Thus: $i - 0.48i = 0.52i$, and $r - 0.48r = 0.52r$.

[p] The mortgage tax credit is 3.5 percent of *gross* income originating from the qualified asset.

Inserting expression (4) into expression (3) yields

$$0.52i + 0.035\bar{\imath} = 0.52(i + X), \text{ or} \qquad (4.13)$$

$$0.035\bar{\imath} = 0.52X; \qquad (4.14)$$

therefore,

$$X = (0.035\bar{\imath})/0.52 \qquad (4.15)$$

Thus, the gross return $\bar{r}$ must be increased by an amount $X = (0.035\bar{\imath}/0.52$ for the aftertax returns on the qualified and nonqualified portfolios to be the same.

As an example, consider a portfolio of qualified assets with a gross rate of return of 8.0 percent. Then, by expression (7), the nonqualified assets must have a gross return of 8.54 percent, or 54 basis points more than the qualified assets, in order to have the same aftertax return. The relevant calculations are shown below, using the notation as defined previously.

$\bar{\imath}$	0.0800
Dividend and interest[a]	0.0640
i	0.0160
Tax	0.0077
After tax income	0.0083
Mortgage tax credit	
$[(0.035)\ (0.08)]$	0.0028
$\underline{\underline{i'}}$	$\underline{\underline{0.0111}}$

The gross interest subsidy necessary to compensate for the mortgage is

$$X = (0.035)\ (0.08)/(0.52) = 0.0054 \qquad (4.16)$$

Therefore:

$\bar{r}$	0.0854
Dividend and interest	0.0640

---

[a] An 80 percent pay-out in interest and dividends assumed. This ratio was 79 percent for S&Ls in 1974.

r	0.0214
Tax	0.0103
$\underline{\underline{r'}}$	$\underline{\underline{0.0111}}$

The average return on qualified assets in S&L portfolios is currently between 6.5 and 7.0 percent. Allowing for the upper limit and assuming that all S&L portfolios qualify for the full mortgage credit,[r] then the proposed 3.5 percent mortgage tax credit constitutes a 47 basis point subsidy to mortgage interest. Even if we allow for growth of returns on mortgages to 8 percent due to continued high long-term rates, the tax subsidy amounts to a 54 basis point increase in return on these mortgages. Given, then, that the mortgage tax credit would provide a subsidy to interest on qualified mortgages somewhere in the vicinity of 50 basis points, what can be said about its impact on home mortgage markets? We can obtain some feel for the relative importance of the subsidy toward stimulating flows of residential mortgage funds through the following analysis.

The problem of funds shortages for single-family home mortgages appears to be a consequence of two different, although not entirely unrelated, events. The first is the inferiority of savings deposits as financial assets during boom periods. During periods of tight credit in which short-term rates rise abnormally high, disintermediation occurs as depositors seek the highest possible market return. These outflows of funds from thrift institutions are a consequence of regulatory constraint on their ability to bid for funds; namely, Regulation Q ceilings which restrict the ability of savings deposit interest rates to float up with other rates.

The other aspect of the problem of funds flows for residential housing arises from the fact that these mortgages have become inferior investment instruments for financial intermediaries in terms of return. It is here that the mortgage tax credit promises to make a "correction" in order to provide adequate funds for housing.

Figures 4–1 and 4–2 show the yield differentials over time between yields on new conventional first-mortgage loans and yields on new Aaa utility bonds, and between yields on the new

---

[r] A reasonable assumption in light of the current composition of S&L portfolios.

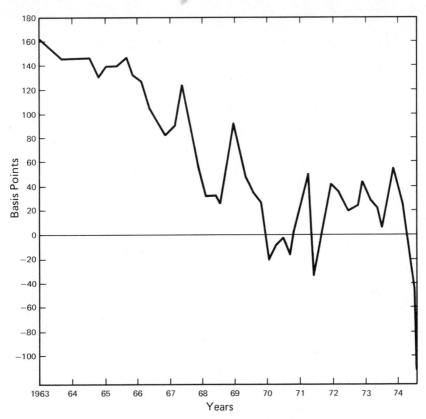

Figure 4–1. Yield Spreads Between FHLBB Conventional First Mortgages[a] and New Aaa Utility Bonds; in Basis Points, 1963–1974[b]

conventional mortgages and those on new mortgage commitments of income property of life insurance companies, respectively.[s] As indicated in these figures, the contract rate yield on conventional, first-mortgage loans for the purchase of single-family homes has steadily deteriorated over the past decade vis-à-vis yields on Aaa (new) utility bonds and LIAA income property yields. In 1963, conventional mortgages held a 160 basis point advantage over new

---

[s] LIAA income property figures are mortgage contract rates on new mortgage commitments of $100,000 or more on multifamily, commercial, industrial, and institutional properties of 15 life insurance companies representing 55 percent of all nonfarm mortgages held by U.S. life insurance companies. Being contract rates, these figures do not reflect "equity kickers" or "pieces of the action," which would add anywhere from 25 to 150 basis points to the existing spread between FHLBB conventionals.

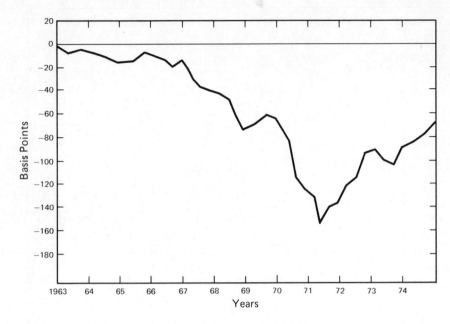

Figure 4–2. Yield Spreads Between FHLBB Conventional First Mortgages[a] and LIAA Income Property;[b] in Basis Points, 1963–1974[c]

issue Aaa utility bonds. As of September 1974, the spread in favor of conventionals had dissipated into a 120 basis point spread advantage to Aaa securities,[t] a swing of nearly 3 percentage points.

The spread between yields on conventional mortgages and LIAA income property has been negative during the sixties and the seventies, although up until 1966 the spread was never more than 10 to 15 basis points. After 1966, the spread began to widen considerably, reaching a difference of nearly 160 basis points in 1971,

---

[t] It could be argued that the "proper" comparison is between FHLBB conventionals and some lower-grade security, since an examination of the portfolios of commercial banks, mutual savings banks, and life insurance companies indicates their average long-term corporate security having a rating between Baa and Aaa. For our purposes here, however, the relevant question is which grade security best represents an equal-risk choice as an investment compared to a conventional mortgage. Because of the relatively low risk nature of the conventional mortgage, we would argue that the best yield comparison is with Aaa utilities (new issues). Regardless, the direction of the spreads is the same over time, with the absolute differences obviously adjusted in the negative direction if the comparison is between yields on conventionals and some lower-grade corporate bonds.

Figure 4–3. Life Insurance Companies—Net Investment Flows; Annual Data; 1962–1974

climbing back to a spread of 70 to 75 basis points as of the end of 1974.

The deterioration of the mortgage as an investment instrument vis-à-vis alternative investments due to changes in their relative yield relationships is reflected in funds flows into and out of investment instruments by the major intermediaries. Figures 4–3, 4–4, and 4–5 show annual funds flows between single-family home mortgages and other securities and mortgages, for life insurance companies, mutual savings banks, and commercial banks.

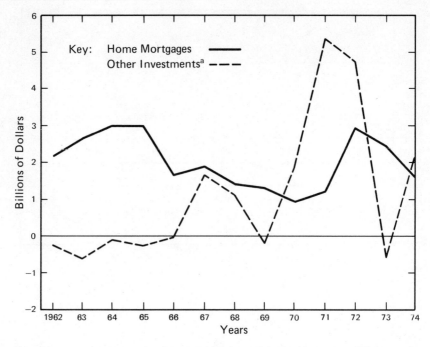

Figure 4–4. Mutual Savings Banks—Net Investment Flows; Annual Data; 1962–1974[a]

Figure 4–3 shows funds flows in home mortgages and other investments for life insurance companies. Since 1966, life insurance companies have actively divested their portfolios of single-family mortgages, moving heavily into commercial property loans and corporate securities. The yield spreads shown in figures 4–1 and 4–2 are consistent with this investment activity by life insurance companies.

Figure 4–4 shows investment flows for mutual savings banks (MSBs). Like those of life insurance companies, these figures reflect a shifting in the allocation of funds, beginning in the 1965–66 period. Whereas funds flows into residential mortgages by MSBs have remained fairly constant over the past decade, acquisition of alternative assets, although volatile, have increased in far greater amounts than home mortgages. Thus, an industry whose primary asset has historically been single-family mortgages has, since 1965,

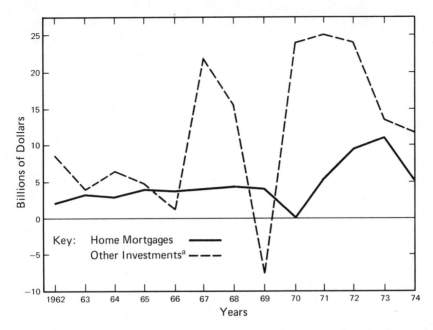

Figure 4–5. Commercial Banks—Net Investment Flows; Annual Data; 1962–1974

increased its holding of such mortgages by only 40 percent, compared to increases in holdings of corporate and state and local securities by over 300 percent.

Figure 4–5 indicates that acquisitions of home mortgages by commercial banks were close to bank acquisitions of financial securities and other mortgages up to 1966. Since that time, banks, like MSBs, have acquired corporate and government securities and other mortgages at a faster rate than single-family mortgages.[2]

These data bear directly on the question of whether the mortgage tax credit of the Financial Institutions Act will provide an "adequate flow of funds into residential housing." Obviously, the answer to this depends upon one's notion of "adequate." If this means a return to pre-1966 conditions—as suggested by Opper in her analysis of the cost of a yield supplement program for home mortgages[3]—then the 3.5 percent mortgage tax credit is insufficient. Our calculations have shown that, based upon current returns on fully qualified portfolios, the mortgage tax credit would provide about a 47 to 53 basis point subsidy to home mortgages. In light of figures 4–1 and 4–2, and based upon the experience of the 1970s to date, this would fail to bring the yield spreads back to 1965 levels.[u] Added to this are two further concerns. First, based upon current portfolios of the major intermediaries that deal in home mortgages, only S&Ls would qualify for the full 3.5 percent credit under the provisions of the Financial Institutions Act. Accordingly, the mortgage interest subsidy to these other intermediaries would be somewhat less than 50 basis points. Secondly, the primary reason as to why S&Ls continue to place most of their funds into home mortgages appears to be the stringent regulations to which these institutions are subject. Under the Financial Institutions Act, the investment powers of S&Ls are to be broadened considerably. In view of recent activities of other financial institutions which are not regulated as narrowly as S&Ls (such as MSBs) one would expect S&Ls to diversify and, in so doing, to decrease their acquisitions of home mortgages.

In conclusion, we would argue that the claim by the treasury that the proposed 3.5 percent mortgage tax credit is going to guarantee sufficient funds flows for housing is open to question and certainly is in need of supporting evidence. Our analysis, although at a preliminary level, fails to support this claim.

---

[u] Particularly in view of our earlier comments as to matters of "equity kickers" and compensating balances associated with commercial property mortgages and business loans.

5 Summary and Conclusions

In the previous chapters, we have developed a picture of the changing structure of federal taxation and regulation among competing intermediaries in general and within the savings and loan industry in particular. The ensuing conclusions and summary statements therefore are based upon what we know about the current tax and regulatory picture for thrifts vis-à-vis banks and what we consider to be reasonable forecasts of future developments in the area of federal taxation as it would impact these intermediaries.

The Bad-Debt Deduction

The tax-saving value of the principal tax avoidance mechanism available to thrift institutions, namely the percentage-of-taxable-income method of calculating bad-debt deductions, has been steadily decreasing since the Tax Reform Act of 1969. As our analysis indicates, the value of this tax avoidance tool to thrift institutions has been further eroded by the impact of the minimum tax, which was initiated in the 1969 Tax Act. Prior to 1969, savings and loan associations were paying federal taxes at rates between 16 and 18 percent, whereas mutual savings banks remained virtually tax exempt. By 1979, our analysis reveals, savings and loans will be paying federal taxes at rates between 24 to 30 percent of their economic income, under the assumption that the current regulatory and tax structures continue to that time. Our figures show that among savings and loans, the larger associations will be paying at the higher rates, approximating 30 percent. By comparison, commercial banks are currently paying federal taxes at rates in the 16 to 18 percent range, although for most of the large banks this figure is lower, even when allowances are made for foreign tax payments. Because tax avoidance by banks is essentially a function of their wide range of investment activities, it is impossible to forecast 1979 tax rate levels. However, based upon what we know about current investment activities and trends among banks, it is quite probable that these rates will be even lower by 1979 than they are presently.

Our analysis shows that the federal tax picture for savings and loans may further deteriorate when consideration is given to the existing limits on the percentage-of-taxable-income method of calculating bad-debt reserve deductions; that is, the so-called "6 percent fill-up" limitation. For example, our simulations have shown that under slow growth situations (similar to the 1969–70 and 1974 periods), the 6 percent ceiling would become effective for large numbers of associations, eliminating this tax shelter provision entirely. Accordingly, average effective federal tax rates for the industry could climb into the 30 to 35 percent range under such slow growth situations.

When consideration is given to regulatory differences between banks and thrift institutions, the differences in effective tax burdens, as calculated by conventional means, are widened. That is, when one imputes into economic income differences in regulatory costs and benefits, then existing differences in effective tax rate calculations are widened in favor of that of banks over both savings and loans and mutual savings banks. Given these considerations, effective tax rate calculations that include both regulatory and tax differences could result in a 20 percentage point advantage to commercial banks over savings and loans by 1980 unless changes are made in the federal taxation or regulation of these intermediaries.

As currently structured, the bad-debt deduction is an institutional (or industry) subsidy and, accordingly, is a prime target for tax reform. Recent history has shown that those tax subsidies that benefit only one or two industries have come under increased scrutiny, as well they should. More and more industry groups which benefit from special tax privileges are being called upon to justify the continuation or existence of these privileges. Like the depletion allowance for the oil industry, the bad-debt deduction is coming under increased criticism as nothing but a pure industry subsidy which has little social benefit. Under any future tax reform package, there will be efforts made by the Congress to continue the process that began in the Revenue Act of 1962 of reducing the bad-debt allowance for thrift institutions. One indirect way in which this may come about is through some increase in the minimum tax on corporations. Our own analysis (as well as that of other researchers in the area of federal taxation) indicates that the bad-debt allowance is a rather inefficient subsidy which makes little economic sense. It is not a cost-effective way to subsidize homes or home mortgages; there is virtually no relation between reserve additions and actual loss experiences; and, it is procyclical in that it subsidizes most during "boom periods" when it is needed the least and subsidizes least during "bust periods" when it is needed the most.

As we have stressed, commercial banks are unable to avail themselves of the same methods for calculating additions to their bad-debt reserves as are thrift institutions, yet we have seen that banks can reduce their effective tax burdens quite successfully by reaping scale economies with respect to asset acquisition, with virtually no help from the Tax Code in the way of privileges reserved exclusively for banks. For example, banks reduce their taxes by leasing operations, yet tax privileges associated with leasing are not restricted to banks. Even the privilege of deducting interest payments associated with the purchase of tax-exempt securities is not strictly limited to commercial banks.

In sum, there seems to be little doubt that the continuation of the bad-debt deduction, as currently structured, is going to result in progressively higher federal taxes for savings and loans and a worsening of their competitive position vis-à-vis that of commercial banks. Accordingly, savings and loans can be expected to turn away from residential mortgages for tax-avoidance purposes, even more so if their investment powers are broadened and the existing tax system remains unchanged.

The Mortgage Tax Credit

The notion of a tax subsidy based upon holdings of residential mortgages, as has been proposed in various versions of financial reform legislation, is more viable economically than is the bad-debt deduction tax subsidy. The mortgage tax credit would be counter-cyclical in that it would provide the greatest amount of subsidy to the industry in periods when the need for loanable funds is greatest. However, as we stressed in an earlier chapter, there is considerable controversy as to whether or not the mortgage tax credit will significantly increase the flow of funds into housing or prevent the divestiture of residential mortgages by savings and loans once they have obtained increased investment powers. Much needed research is yet to be done on this matter.[1]

In addition, the concept of a mortgage interest tax credit is consistent with the savings and loan industry's remaining specialists as intermediaries in residential mortgages. However, as has been pointed out by several researchers in this area, it is this very notion that conflicts with the basic goal of the Hunt Commission (the foundation of the Financial Institutions Act): an increase in competition among financial intermediaries.[2]

Based upon these thoughts and our findings on the mortgage tax credit in previous chapters, we note the following provisos regarding this proposed change in the tax treatment of financial institutions:

1. If adopted, the mortgage tax credit should not be determined strictly on the basis of an equal tax-dollar trade with the existing bad-debt allowance, as has been suggested in previous reform proposals. There is no rationale for this position on equity, neutrality, or any other grounds.

2. On pure equity grounds between competing intermediaries, the mortgage tax credit should compensate for any differences that exist between thrifts and commercial banks as a consequence of existing federal tax and regulatory structures. In point of fact, however, it is virtually impossible to recommend any tax program that is going to settle such an equity problem for any lengthy period of time. Commercial bank taxes are heavily contingent upon their investment activities. Our analysis has shown that taxes for savings and loans under the mortgage tax credit would be quite sensitive to both short- and long-term interest rates. Accordingly, equity, once achieved, may well be short-lived.

This is not to dismiss the tax fairness issues. However, the best that may be possible in the name of tax equity among competing financial intermediaries is a periodic adjustment or "correction" in the Tax Code, such as took place in 1962 and again in 1969. Developments since the 1969 Tax Reform Act indicate that such an adjustment on equity grounds is again needed, particularly when a more global view of taxation is taken within the context of regulatory differences. Our analysis has shown that the 3.5 percent mortgage tax credit, as proposed by both the Nixon and Ford administrations, would at least partially correct for some of the differences that currently exist in the comparative federal tax and regulatory burdens of commercial banks and savings and loans. (Recall that in chapter 4 we showed that in all but the most extreme circumstances, the 3.5 percent mortgage tax credit would more than compensate savings and loans for loss of the percentage-of-taxable-income method of calculating bad-debt reserve deductions.) In light of the nature of the mortgage tax credit and its availability to commercial banks, our figures suggest that a similarly structured credit with a ceiling of 4.0 percent, rather than 3.5 percent, would in an average performance year[a] for savings and loans bring the effective tax rates of S&Ls more closely in line with those of commercial banks.[b]

3. The Treasury claims that the mortgage tax credit should be sufficient to induce savings and loans, and other intermediaries, to hold residential mortgages without the added force of regulation. But in view of our analysis in chapter 4, and based on the findings of other researchers whom we have cited from time to time throughout the text, we must question this contention. We have shown that the credit as proposed would constitute about a 50 basis point subsidy to home mortgages. In light of the deterioration of returns on home mortgages vis-à-vis alternative investment instruments over the past decade, a 50 basis point boost for mortgages is not going to place them in the same competitive position that they enjoyed prior to 1966. This suggests a mortgage tax credit higher than 3.5 percent, but a little reflection would indicate this to be a stopgap action at best. First, the cost to the Treasury of a long-term credit in the 6 to 7 percent range would be prohibitive. The Treasury conservatively estimates an annual net revenue loss under the Senate-proposed 3.8 percent credit in excess of $850 million by 1980. Second, credits of this size would virtually eliminate tax payment by thrifts and commercial banks. This sort of thing is not likely to be tolerated by the Congress.

Finally, the first two points suggest that the market inferiority of mortgages is not going to be solved through the tax system.

---

[a] Average in terms of net return, based on the savings and loan industry's record over the past 5 years.

[b] These rates having been adjusted for existing regulatory differences, as developed in chapter 3. In addition, we are assuming that effective tax rates for banks stabilize at present levels.

Long-run solutions to this problem are going to require a restructuring of either home mortgage markets or the home mortgage itself—such as through the variable rate mortgage concept.

4. If enacted, the mortgage tax credit should be structured in order to permit rebates, as in the form of a negative income tax. Failure to enact a provision of this nature subjects the mortgage tax subsidy to the same criticism as the bad-debt deduction; that is, the value of the subsidy may be reduced because of insufficient income—yet this is when the subsidy is needed most. In addition, rebates would draw nontaxable intermediaries, like pension funds, and low tax-rate units, like life insurance companies, more into the mortgage markets. Carry-back and carry-forward provisions are likely to prove inadequate in this regard.

There are two specific implications of this analysis for public policy. First of all, the regulatory system, weighing more heavily on the major housing lenders in the economy, has a dampening impact on the housing market. To the extent that the power of thrifts to compete with commercial banks for funds is constrained, the flow of funds into housing is diminished. Secondly, the evidence presented here bears on the impact of the current proposals for the reform of the financial sector. The Financial Institutions Act, as passed by the Senate, would remove much of the differential impact of the regulatory system by extending both the asset and liability powers of thrifts. Our analysis suggests that this extension of powers would enable thrifts to compete more strongly for funds and would increase the flow of funds into housing.

The currently proposed legislation for financial reform includes provisions of one type or another for changes in the tax treatment of intermediaries. These programs attempt to present an integrated package of tax and regulatory reform, and, as such, recognize the essential tax and subsidy elements in regulation. The mortgage tax credit, in and of itself, would do little in the way of reforming the financial system or solving the recurrent problems that plague the housing industry. Problems of disintermediation, shortages of mortgage money at reasonable rates, and wide fluctuations in the rate of housing starts, require dealing with such questions as the elimination of Regulation Q, increased portfolio powers for thrift institutions, and the institution of the variable-rate mortgage. As a temporary measure, the mortgage tax credit would be an improvement over the existing tax treatment of thrift institutions, but in no way would it solve all equity and neutrality questions surrounding the taxation and regulation of financial institutions. The politics of the situation seem to suggest that financial reform is not likely to get off the ground unless some sort of direct or indirect home mortgage subsidy is included. Because of the pressing need and potential social benefits of financial reform in those areas suggested by the Hunt Commission, this alone might be worth the price of the mortgage tax credit.

Notes

Notes

Chapter 2
Issues in the Current Tax Treatment of Savings and
Loan Associations

1. For documentation as to these investments and their contributions to the tax reduction of commercial banks, see Kenneth R. Biederman and John A. Tuccillo, *The Taxation and Regulation of Commercial Banks* (Washington, D.C.: National Savings and Loan League, December 1974).

2. See Biederman and Tuccillo, *Taxation and Regulation of Commercial Banks*, pp. 12–25.

3. See Edward J. Kane, "Federal Income-Tax Burdens of Commercial Banks and Savings and Loan Associations," Federal Home Loan Bank Board *Journal*, July 1973, pp. 10–17.

4. See Kenneth R. Biederman and John A. Tuccillo, *The Taxation and Regulation of Mutual Savings Banks* (Washington, D.C.: National Savings and Loan League, April 1975), p. 18, for detailed analysis.

5. See Biederman and Tuccillo, *Taxation and Regulation of Commercial Banks*, pp. 26–39, 52–57.

6. Both of these issues are particularly applicable to commercial banks and are discussed in Biederman and Tuccillo, *Taxation and Regulation of Commercial Banks*, pp. 46–57.

7. Kane underscores the notion of the Federal Reserve using various instruments of monetary policy, such as reserve requirements, in a fashion and with the effects of taxation and subsidization. E. J. Kane, "All for the Best: The Federal Reserve Board's *60th Annual Report*," in *The American Economic Review*, LXIV (December 1974), pp. 835–850.

Chapter 3
The Income Effects of Regulation within the Savings
and Loan Industry

1. D. D. Hester, *Stock and Mutual Associations in the Savings and Loan Industry* (Washington, D.C.: Federal Home Loan Bank Board, 1967).

2. Ibid., pp. 16–17, cites the more personal stake of management as the reason for expecting stocks to be more aggressive.

3. Kane and Valentini, "Tax Avoidance by Savings and Loan Associations."

4. Ibid.

5. This method is straightforward and has been used in a number of other similar contexts. See American Bankers Association, *Toward A More Viable Financial Sector*, 1971, pp. 68–69; J. F. Gatti, "Expanded Deposit Powers for Thrift Institutions" (Federal Reserve Bank of Boston, unpublished, 1970); and L. Lapidus, *Public Policy Towards Mutual Savings Banks in New York State: Proposals for Change* (Federal Reserve Bank of New York, 1974), Ch. 6.

6. American Bankers Association, *Toward A More Viable Financial Sector*.

7. Vernon's estimate lies in the upper part of this range (78 basis points) while the Friend study uses the entire range. See Jack R. Vernon, "Competition for Savings Deposits: The Recent Experience," *National Banking Review*, December 1966; and *Study of the Savings and Loan Industry*, Federal Home Loan Bank Board, 1969, Vol. III.

8. Lapidus, *Public Policy Towards Mutual Savings Banks*, chapter 6.

9. Sandra B. Cohan, "Competitive Position of Commercial Banks vis-à-vis Mutual Savings Banks in Massachusetts," FDIC Working Paper #72-15. The paper addressed itself to mutual savings banks in Massachusetts.

10. The prime reference in this field is C. F. Haywood, *The Pledging of Bank Assets* (Chicago: Association of Reserve City Bankers, 1967); see also, J. A. Verbrugge and C. F. Haywood, "Secured Public Deposits and the Interests of Banks, Public Agencies and Unsecured Depositors," *Quarterly Review of Economics and Business* (Summer 1970); and J. E. Peterson, *Full Insurance of Public Deposits and Pledging Requirements* (Washington, D.C.: Municipal Finance Officers Association, February 1, 1974). A comprehensive study is currently being conducted by Dr. Charles Hempel for the Advisory Commission on Intergovernmental Relations.

11. Haywood, *Pledging of Bank Assets.*

12. Petersen, *Full Insurance of Public Deposits.*

13. Ibid.

14. The derivation of these figures, accompanied by discussion and analysis of methodology, can be found in Biederman and Tuccillo, *Taxation and Regulation of Commercial Banks,* pp. 79–105; and Biederman and Tuccillo, *Taxation and Regulation of Mutual Savings Banks,* pp. 20–52.

15. Patric Hendershott, "The Impact of the Financial Institutions Act" (Mimeographed, August 1975).

Chapter 4
The Mortgage Tax Credit

1. Kenneth R. Biederman, John A. Tuccillo, and George J. Viksnins, *A Comparison of the Current Bad Debt Allowance and the Proposed Mortgage Tax Credit Provisions* (Washington, D.C.: National Savings and Loan League), 1974.

2. Barbara Opper has shown a similar development since 1965 in looking at net loans to business vs. funds flows by banks into home mortgages. See: Barbara Negri Opper, "Interest Equalization on Home Mortgages," in *Ways to Moderate Fluctuations in Housing Construction,* Federal Reserve Staff Study, Washington, D.C., December 1972, pp. 322–336; in particular, see p. 325.

3. See Opper, *Ways to Moderate Fluctuations,* pp. 328 ff.

Chapter 5
Summary and Conclusions

1. Fair and Jaffee, making comparative simulation experiments using MIT-FRB-Penn Econometric Model, have shown that direct subsidies for housing are more efficient than direct subsidies for mortgages in stimulating housing investment. Ray C. Fair and Dwight W. Jaffee, "The Implications of the Proposals of the Hunt Commission for the Mortgage and Housing Markets: An Empirical Study," *Policies for a More Competitive Financial System: A*

Review of the President's Commission on Financial Structure and Regulation, Conference Series No. 8, Federal Reserve Bank of Boston, 1972, p. 129.

2. For example, see Edward J. Kane, "Costs and Benefits of the Proposed Tax Credit on Residential-Mortgage Income," *Journal of Bank Research, 6,* No. 2 (Summer 1975): pp. 88–99.

Bibliography

Bibliography

Bell, Fredrick W., and Neil B. Murphy. *Costs in Commercial Banking*. Boston: Federal Reserve Bank of Boston, 1968.

Biederman, Kenneth R. *Federal Income Taxation of the Savings and Loan and Commercial Banking Industries*. Washington, D.C.: National League of Insured Savings Associations, 1973.

Biederman, Kenneth R., and John A. Tuccillo. *Equity Issues As They Relate to the Savings and Loan Industry*. Washington, D.C.: National Savings and Loan League, 1974.

―――. *The Taxation and Regulation of Commercial Banks*. Washington, D.C.: National Savings and Loan League, 1974.

―――. *The Taxation and Regulation of Mutual Savings Banks*. Washington, D.C.: National Savings and Loan League, 1975.

Biederman, Kenneth R., Gary Robbins, and Emil M. Sunley, Jr. "A Comparison of Various Proposals for a Minimum Tax and Allocation of Deductions." *Proceedings of the 69th Annual Conference on Taxation*, 1971, pp. 148–178.

Biederman, Kenneth R., John A. Tuccillo, and George J. Viksnins. *A Comparison of the Bad Debt Allowance and the Proposed Mortgage Tax Credit*. Washington, D.C.: National Savings and Loan League, 1974.

Bond, Richard E. "Deposit Composition and Commercial Bank Earnings." Unpublished Ph.D. dissertation, University of Maryland, 1969.

Buek, R. W., Jr. *An Analysis of the Foreign Tax Credit: Per Country and Overall Limitations*. Washington, D.C.: U.S. Chamber of Commerce, 1974.

Cohan, Sandra B. "The Competitive Position of Commercial Banks Vis-à-Vis Mutual Savings Banks in Massachusetts," Working Paper #72-15, Federal Deposit Insurance Corporation, Washington, D.C., 1972.

Cox, Albert H., Jr. *Regulation of Interest on Bank Deposits*. Ann Arbor, Mich.: University of Michigan Bureau of Business Research, 1966.

Federal Deposit Insurance Corporation. *Annual Report,* Washington, D.C., 1971–1974.

————. *Assets and Liabilities of Commercial and Mutual Savings Banks,* Washington, D.C., December 31, 1973.

Federal Savings and Loan Insurance Corporation. *Combined Financial Statements—FSLIC Insured Savings and Loan Associations,* Washington, D.C., 1971–1974.

Friend, Irwin, ed. "Changes in the Asset and Liability Structure of the Savings and Loan Industry." In *Study of the Savings and Loan Industry.* Washington, D.C.: Federal Home Loan Bank Board, 1969, pp. 1355–1433.

Gallagher, Thomas J., Jr. "Tax Consequences of a Leveraged Lease Transaction," *Taxes,* June 1974, pp. 356–364.

Gatti, James F. "Expanded Deposit Powers for Thrift Institutions," Federal Reserve Bank of Boston, 1970. (Mimeographed.)

Halperin, Daniel I. "Federal Income Taxation of Banks," *Proceedings of the 69th Annual Conference on Taxation,* 1971, pp. 318–334.

Haywood, Charles F. *The Pledging of Bank Assets.* Chicago: Association of Reserve City Bankers, 1967.

————, and James F. Verbrugge. "Secured Public Deposits and the Interests of Banks, Public Agencies and Unsecured Depositors," *Quarterly Review of Economics and Business,* Summer 1970.

Hendershott, Patric H. "The Impact of the Financial Institutions Act," Department of Housing and Urban Development, Washington, D.C., August 1975. (Mimeographed.)

Hester, Donald D. *Stock and Mutual Associations in the Savings and Loan Industry.* Washington, D.C.: Federal Home Loan Bank Board, 1967.

Jacobs, Donald. *Business Loan Costs and Bank Market Structure.* New York: National Bureau of Economic Research, 1971.

Kane, Edward J. "All for the Best: The Federal Reserve Board's 60th *Annual Report,*" *American Economic Review,* LXIV (December 1974), 835–850.

————. "Federal Income Tax Burdens of Commercial Banks and Savings and Loan Associations," Federal Home Loan Bank Board *Journal* (July 1973), pp. 10–17.

Kane, Edward J., and John Valentini. "Tax Avoidance by Savings and Loan Associations Before and After the Tax Reform Act of 1969," *Journal of Monetary Economics,* I, No. 1 (January 1975), pp. 41–64.

Lapidus, Leonard. *Public Policy Toward Mutual Savings Banks in New York State: Proposals for Reform.* Federal Reserve Bank of New York, 1974.

Lawrence, Robert J. "Operating Policies of Bank Holding Companies—Part I," Staff Economic Study #59. Washington, D.C.: Board of Governors of the Federal Reserve System, 1971.

————. "Operating Policies of Bank Holding Companies—Part II," Staff Economic Study #81. Washington, D.C.: Board of Governors of the Federal Reserve System, 1974.

McCoy, J., and C. W. Schoeneman. "Bad Debt Reserves of Financial Institutions," *William and Mary Law Review* (Summer 1970), pp. 797–840.

McGugan, Vincent J. *Competition and Adjustment in the Equipment Leasing Industry.* Research Report #51. Boston: Federal Reserve Bank of Boston, 1972.

Mullineaux, Donald J. "Taxman Rebuffed: Income Taxes at Commercial Banks," Federal Reserve Bank of Philadelphia *Business Review* (May 1974).

Opper, Barbara N. "Interest Equalization on Home Mortgages." In *Ways to Moderate Fluctuations in Housing Construction.* Washington, D.C.: Board of Governors of the Federal Reserve System, 1972, pp. 322–336.

Peterson, John E. *Full Insurance of Public Deposits and Pledging Requirements.* Washington, D.C.: Municipal Finance Officers' Association, 1974.

Piper, Thomas, and Stephen Weiss. "Profitability of Bank Acquisitions by Multi-Bank Holding Companies," *New England Economic Review* (September 1971), pp. 3–12.

Rosenblum, Harvey. "Bank Holding Companies: An Overview," Federal Reserve Bank of Chicago *Business Conditions* (August 1973), pp. 1–8.

Schweiger, I., and J. McGee. "Chicago Banking," *Journal of Business* (July 1961), pp. 311–335.

Shull, Bernard, and Paul Horvitz. "Branch Banking and the Structure of Competition," *National Banking Review* (March 1964), pp. 301–341.

———. "The Impact of Branch Banking on Performance," *National Banking Review* (December 1964).

Stafford, John. "An Analysis of the Treasury's Proposed Interest Rate Credit Versus the Bad Debt Method of Taxation of Savings Associations." Chicago: U.S. League of Savings Associations, 1973. (Mimeographed.)

Talley, Samuel H. "The Impact of Holding Company Acquisition on Concentration in Banking." Staff Economic Study #80. Washington, D.C.: Board of Governors of the Federal Reserve System, 1974.

Tax Notes. Washington, D.C.: Tax Analysts and Advocates, December 24, 1973.

Teck, Alan. *Mutual Savings Banks and Savings and Loan Associations: Aspects of Growth.* New York: Columbia University Press, 1968.

Toward A More Viable Financial System. Washington, D.C.: American Bankers' Association, 1971.

Treasury Department. *Short Summary of the Financial Institutions Act of 1973,* Washington, D.C., 1973.

———. *Tax Reform Studies and Proposals.* Hearings before the U.S. House of Representatives, Committee on Ways and Means, 91st Congress, First Session, Washington, D.C., 1969.

———, Internal Revenue Service. *Recommendations for Change in the U.S. Financial System,* Washington, D.C., 1973.

———. *Statements of Income —Corporate Source Book,* Washington, D.C., 1970–72.

Vernon, Jack R. "Competition for Savings Deposits: The Recent Experience," *National Banking Review* (December 1966).

Weiss, Stephen, and Vincent J. McGugan. "The Equipment Leasing Industry and the Emerging Role of Banking Organizations," *New England Economic Review* (November 1973), pp. 3–30.

Index

Index

American Bankers' Association, 48, 65

Bad Debt Deduction, assets qualifying under, 8; decreases in allowable percentage, 5–8; impact on assets, 8–10; impact on six percent accumulation limit, 11–16; limitations, 7–8; method of calculation, 28n; relation to mortgage tax credit, 67–70; conclusions concerning, 91–93

Economic Income, and regulation, 37–38; definition, 2, 6n; and tax equity, 31

Federal Deposit Insurance Corporation, 2, 37
Federal Home Loan Bank Board, 2, 4, 37, 54, 55
Federal Reserve System, 2, 37, 52, 65n
Financial Institutions Act, 2, 4, 65, 65n, 66, 66n, 94, 96

Minimum Tax, and neutral tax credit, 16n; definition, 16; equalization of base, 16–19; impact on asset selection, 20–27; impact on effective tax rates, 16–20; legislative history, 19–20; potential changes, 31n; summary of analysis, 28–29
Mortgage Tax Credit, 65–90; aggregate comparison with bad debt deduction, 78–81; conclusions concerning, 93–97; future tax burdens under, 72–76; and housing, 81–90; impact on cyclical income behavior, 76–77; and minimum tax, 70–72; qualifying assets under, 65–66; rate of credit, 66; relation to bad debt deduction, 67–70

Organizational Form of Savings and Loan Associations, 39–48; American Bankers' Association position, 48n; comparative operating procedures, 42–45; comparative tax burdens, 44–47; mutual vs. stock balance sheet and size comparisons, 39–42; subsidy to mutuals, 47–48

Presidential Commission on Financial Structure and Regulation (Hunt Commission), xv, 1, 65, 65n, 94, 97
Public Unit Accounts, 55–60; at commercial banks, 56–57; deposit insurance limits, 55–56; and financial markets, 57–58; and thrifts, 58–60

Regulation, costs and benefits of, 3–4, 33–36, 37–39, 49–64; and alternative borrowing sources, 54–55; and differential reserve requirements, 51–54; impact of prohibition of full services to thrifts, 49–51; impact on tax rates, 60–64
Regulation Q, 49, 50, 96
Revenue Act of 1951, 5
Revenue Act of 1962, xv, 5–6, 31, 32, 92, 94

Section 593, 22, 23, 24

Tax Equity, 29–36; and deficiencies of effective rate measures, 32–33; and economic income, 29–31; and portfolio flexibility, 31–32; and regulation, 33–36, 60–64·
Tax Reform Act of 1969, xv, 4, 6–8, 9n, 15, 20, 24, 29, 31, 32, 58, 91, 94

113

About the Authors

Kenneth R. Biederman is Senior Vice President, Economics and Planning, at City Federal Savings and Loan, Elizabeth, New Jersey. Prior to this, he was with the Office of Tax Analysis, U.S. Treasury Department, and was a staff economist with the U.S. Senate Budget Committee. From 1971–1975, Dr. Biederman served on the faculty of the Department of Economics, Georgetown University.

John A. Tuccillo is a Brookings Economic Policy Fellow at the Department of Housing and Urban Development. Since 1971, he has been an assistant professor of economics at Georgetown University.

The authors recently co-authored a five volume study on the taxation and regulation of financial institutions, commissioned by the National Savings and Loan League.